"Stu brings into any org. ... s a **common language** for e ... our *People You Should Know* becomes the standard terminology your team will utilize not only in selling to prospective clients but selling internally as well. Personally, as an 'Orange,' I can't recommend him more!"

Ivan G. Boyd, Senior VP, and CRO
GTESS Corporation

"Stu's practical approach to improving communications isn't just for salespeople. We've **applied it with great success** to improve the interaction of a large project team too. The all too typical situation of different people having different definitions of success was making communication, and progress, rather frustrating for everyone. Stu showed us how to identify the real needs and priorities of each member of the team and then how to communicate with each of them every day focusing on exactly what was important to them. **The difference is amazing**—everyone is now pulling in the same direction, and most importantly, each person thinks 'color' first, to keep communications running smoothly every day. Stu's methodology is now part of the way we do business!"

Barbara Lancaster
President, LTC International, Inc.

"Stu is one gifted teacher who can **bring across his ideas very succinctly and clearly to his audience.** His stint in Singapore was certainly a very memorable time for our industry. All the participants gave him a 'thumbs-up' for his sessions. They benefited greatly from his training and found the ideas about the four kinds of people 'revealing.'

I would certainly recommend Stu to any companies who want to **boost the performance of their salespeople.** Please book him now!"

Samuel Goh-Former President
Financial Services Management Association—Singapore

"I saw Stu Schlackman speak at MDRT in Anaheim where he presented to approximately 1000 members and received an outstanding response from everyone in the room. **Stu's presentation style is both entertaining and very informative.** Stu received a lot of questions following his presentation, which is always a good sign that the audience were engaged and wanting more."

Ross Hultgren
Financial Planner
MDRT Australia, Chairman

"Without a doubt, Stu Schlackman is one of **the most informative and inspiring instructors available today.** Altogether with his Personality Assessment, the Sales Leadership and Relationship Building sessions delivered for our clients were well structured with relevant exercises. I would strongly recommend Stu's training workshops to help **improve leadership abilities and management skills."**

Michael McGowan
President, The McGowan Team

"Stu's unique personality assessment is easy and fun, and **helps teams understand the unique strengths** that they and their colleagues bring to the table. His program has helped our associates to improve communication and collaboration with one another, harness the power of their own preferred working styles, and appreciate the ways in which **diverse personality types serve to strengthen our organization.**

I highly recommend Stu's approach, as it continues to create **a lasting positive impact** on our career development efforts as well as on our company as a whole."

Kerry Hrenko
Vice President, Avenue 5

THE RELATIONSHIP SELLING SECRET

OTHER BOOKS BY STU SCHLACKMAN

Don't Just Stand There, Sell Something

Four People You Should Know

The 180 Rule for the Art of Connecting

From the Star to the Cross

Dinner with a Side of Doubts

The Sales Leader's Guide to Empowering Your Team to Increase Their Influence and Generate More Profitable Connections

THE RELATIONSHIP SELLING SECRET

STU SCHLACKMAN

THE RELATIONSHIP SELLING SECRET

ISBN: 9781956465051

You can find information on Stu Schlackman's workshops, sign up for our newsletter, and order additional books (volume discounts available) at:

StuSchlackman.com

Published in the United States by
Soar 2 Success Publishing

www.Soar2SuccessPublishing.com

TABLE OF CONTENTS

A NOTE FROM STU

In 2004, a good friend of mine showed me a very simple tool to identify someone's Personality Style by selecting a postcard I was drawn to. When I picked the card that I related to, he told me to turn it over and read about that personality type. I was blown away! It described everything about the way I communicate, what I value, and even some of the hobbies that were of interest to me.

As a sales trainer and coach, I thought to myself, why couldn't I use something like this to improve the art of selling and building long-term relationships with customers? If I can identify the personality type of a customer, I thought, I could better connect with them. The results can lead to more new sales, shorter sales cycles, improving salespeople's win rates, and for the sales leader, reduce turnover and build a stronger team.

I started using the personality tool and developed a workshop to help salespeople improve their relationship building with prospects and customers from their perspective. The workshop lasted from two hours to a full day. I received great feedback from clients, especially those in financial services, real estate, and hi-tech, where their sales results saw excellent growth. This is especially true in these industries that have a longer selling cycle, and where relationship building is key.

My good friend Trevor Hayes had helped me write my first book, *Don't Just Stand There, Sell Something,* the year before. As I delivered my workshops using Personality Styles, I began to think about writing another book addressing the elements of relationship selling.

On the way to Italy for a two-week vacation I turned to Trevor and the rest of our company heading for Tuscany, and announced I was going to write a book for salespeople on how to sell to the different Personality Styles. I thought a book addressing the "how to" in sales would help salespeople achieve success from a new perspective.

By the end of our vacation, most of the book was complete. I then sought the support of Trevor and another friend, Wedge Greene, to help fine-tune the book using the content of my workshops.

As a hands-on salesperson who is practical and always asks, "So what," I wanted to have a book that can help salespeople be more successful using my model.

After working with sales teams and Personality Styles for many years now, I saw the need for sales leaders to embrace this approach. I felt almost compelled to address sales leadership with the Four People Personality Styles. In recent years, they have become so focused on the short-term, caring mostly about hitting numbers, rather than developing individuals to achieve more.

I felt and saw their frustration at how bad sales turnover has become. I knew they needed help understanding how to best coach their people. That's why I wrote this book.

The personality tool I developed is sales-focused and will help sales leaders achieve their goals on a more consistent basis.

I've been in sales and sales leadership now for over thirty-five years and truly believe that sales is a competitive sport. I love sports, and I love sales. The goal of both is to win, and I love winning!

Whether you are a leader in sales, or want to become one someday, I believe this book will help you achieve that goal.

FOREWORD
BY SCOTT SCHLACKMAN

I've known Stu Schlackman for a lifetime, obviously, since he's my older brother. What makes our relationship unique is the fact that just over the past few years, we have begun to connect in a way that we never did in our younger days. In fact, up until now the only thing we had in common was our shoe size. He always did things so fast, and I was more cautious. Stu would take risks, while I was careful. I like harmony and he loved when things were chaotic. So as youngsters and throughout our adult lives, we both went our separate ways. However, over the past few years, our relationship has grown both personally and professionally in a way that we would have never imagined.

One would think that our newfound closeness would come about through long discussions and working through our differences. Not at all! After all these years, a light bulb went off, and that light bulb was a Personality Styles tool that my brother developed, which was the major focus in his first book. Thanks to this tool, I now have a much better understanding of my Personality Style and that of my brother's and everyone around me. Understanding our Personality Styles has enabled us to value each other's differences versus having our differences alienate us. Our differences in personality have now bonded us in a way that we would never have imagined.

Stu has extensive experience in sales leadership and has built highly successful teams. Stu's new book you are about to enjoy focuses on different sales leadership styles. My leadership journey over the years has taken a different path than Stu's. I have been traveling the world as a global executive, building teams in fifteen different countries. I've had the opportunity to work in different cultures and languages under complex situations. I have always used my intuitive skills, my gut, to better understand people and help them connect to achieve their goals. While I was successful, I must say that at times it was challenging and at the same time exhausting. Meeting new people in different cultures and trying to understand how and why they tick is not always easy. I always thought there must be an assessment tool that could help people connect. I've tried every tool imaginable available on the marketplace. While many of them are good, I always had a hard time applying them in real-life situations. They were too complex and cumbersome. In today's world, we need speed and tools that are easy to use. I always ended up going back to my gut reaction on how to connect and motivate other people. However, I was always on the lookout for reassurance that my intuition was correct.

While I was out traveling the world, my brother, unbeknownst to me, was developing his personality tool that did everything I was looking for. A tool that could quickly help people better understand their Personality Style and how their style can impact peers and their customers. In addition, it helps sales leaders maximize the strengths of each of the individuals on their team. Stu's tool achieves this goal in ways I never thought possible. It does all of this and at the same time it is easy to use.

What makes this tool so special is that it is simple, easy to understand, and fast to implement. In today's environment, we do not have a second to lose. Stu's personality assessment provides results in ten minutes. Remember, Stu likes to do things fast! While I am a skeptic and prefer to do everything intuitively, I was astounded at how accurate it was while being so quick. It has provided me with an invaluable resource to better understand the teams I'm working with and the individuals I coach. The combination of my brother's tool and my intuition has enabled me to dramatically improve my leadership skills, build teams, and connect so much better with those around me.

What's even more rewarding after all these years, my brother and I have teamed up to produce seminars, coaching and consulting to help sales teams develop exceptional performance. We combine my global experience with his fabulous assessment tool to help sales leaders, individuals, and teams connect to build long-lasting and profitable relationships with customers like never before.

Scott Schlackman
President, Scott Schlackman Global Consulting
Former President, Avon Products—United Kingdom, Continental Europe, Canada, France, and Greece
Board of Directors, Medifast

INTRODUCTION

What is Relationship Selling and Why is it Important

Relationship selling is all about connecting with others on a deeper level. It's putting the other person's perspective as a priority, understanding what's most important to them. Building relationships is for the long-term. It requires building a relationship based on mutual trust, being open and flexible to every possibility that arises. It's a give and take, a balance between the seller and the customer, the sales leader and the salesperson, a husband and a wife, with an understanding of the importance of the relationship.

The Four People Personality Style Assessment

Understanding the four Personality Styles will help you to understand not only *what* is most important to the other person but also *why* it's important to them. It will help you to better identify with how the four styles naturally communicate their needs and desires. It will help you understand how they go about making decisions, whether they make them fast or slow, or with their heart, head, or gut. Each style has a different priority around what they value. Building relationships is about re-aligning our views of situations based on the views of the other person. When we can identify the Personality Style of the other person and understand their needs, we have a much better chance of connecting with them from their perspective.

How Using the Assessment Will Help You Be a Better Sales Leader

The four Personality Styles need to trust in you, the leader. This trust will motivate them to achieve the goals you set for them. Using the assessment will bring clarity to your salespeople in better understanding what your intentions are and why. Your people will understand that your interaction with them is not cookie cutter but unique to their Personality Style to help them maximize their importance. You will know their strengths and where they can improve, and they will trust your advice to achieve the results you have set for them. Using the assessment will help you take your relationship with your salespeople to a deeper level and gain a better understanding of their desires and needs.

How Your Sales Team Can Better Serve Their Prospects and Customers

Using this book will help you address this Personality Style dimension that is often overlooked when we convey our message to customers, team members, and leaders. The reason is because it's natural to view life from our perspective or personality, which is our default way of seeing life.

Post-Pandemic Selling

Of course, we can't go much further without acknowledging COVID-19.

Even though the new decade beginning in 2020 was impacted by the pandemic, we are beginning to move in a more positive direction. As this is written in late 2021, COVID-19 is still impacting society and businesses in many ways. Some world economies have been crushed; businesses have closed, some permanently and others temporarily; and companies have furloughed millions of people. One component of business that needs to adjust is sales. The common face-to-face sales meeting is now more often conducted with online tools like Zoom or Microsoft Teams. To connect and build customer relationships is more challenging. Taking customers out to lunch, dinner, or sports events during the pandemic disappeared overnight. Sales leaders and their people need to be more effective than ever before. We can still identify Personality Styles by what the customer says, we just need to be better listeners.

Another challenge of the pandemic is that it has forced many to work at home. As you'll learn later in this book, this is more acceptable to people who fall under the Gold and Green Personality Styles, as they are more task focused. But for the Blue and Orange styles, being more relationship-focused, they miss the in-person interaction. Change is inevitable in our world and when we consider our Personality Style, it will help us to understand how we respond and adapt to those changes in our business and personal lives.

Now that the challenge of selling remotely is more prevalent, the impact we make on every call with every prospect or customer needs to deliver great value in meeting their needs. Communication and robust dialogue are more critical than ever before.

- ✓ Salespeople need to be more engaging by asking more focused questions of the customer.
- ✓ Advancing the sale must be more deliberate.
- ✓ Conveying value must be the top priority when we are working with customers online.
- ✓ Sales leaders need to coach their salespeople on a more consistent basis.
- ✓ Salespeople need to be disciplined in their daily routine when it comes to prospecting, current sales opportunities, and their pipeline management.
- ✓ Time management is important to stay disciplined.

This book is split into five parts. Below is an overview of what you will learn about in each part.

In Part One:
- ✓ We will explore what personality is and each of the four Personality Styles.
- ✓ The factors to consider are communication, values, conflict, change, stress, and conflict to name a few.
- ✓ We will look at the benefits of understanding personality in our interactions.

In Part Two:
- ✓ We will introduce the Personality Style Assessment.
- ✓ You will find a recap and summary of each of the Personality Styles.

In Part Three:
- ✓ We will go over how the assessment relates to leadership and working with your salespeople.
- ✓ You will learn how it impacts the dynamics of the sales team.

✓ We will also explore how to best manage conflict and stress.

In Part Four:

✓ We will delve further into the Personality Styles.
✓ You will learn how to understand your style and whether or not it changes.
✓ We will go over how to place the right person in the right job.
✓ We will discuss the quadrants of the brain.
✓ We will look at how styles relate to culture, and how styles affect work and play.
✓ You will learn how to use styles with others and how to identify someone else's Personality Style.

In Part Five:

✓ We will explore personality-based selling.
✓ You will learn how to build customer relationships and communicate with the customer.
✓ We will discuss customer buying preferences and how to handle customer objections.
✓ We will go over how to close the deal.
✓ We will conclude with why the Personality Styles aren't just a theory.

As a sales leader, your challenge is leading a team that you may not be seeing in person on a day-to-day basis. More now than ever, your ability to coach and connect is paramount. It's critical to understand the needs of your people and to relate to them from their personality perspective. We will address the needs of your people and help you take care of them, since they are the number one asset of your team.

This book provides the secret to relationship selling by introducing Personality Styles. It aims to help you apply your new understanding of the four styles to achieve results in the practical world of selling and sales leadership by building stronger and more profitable relationships. If you're a sales leader or aspiring to be a leader, a new salesperson or a seasoned one, this book will increase your success.

"YOUR
ABILITY TO
COACH
AND
CONNECT
IS PARAMOUNT"

We will explore many key elements of interacting with others—whether it's in professional or personal situations. We will look at how each personality makes decisions, especially buying decisions. We will examine the different personalities' attitudes and behavior with respect to change, conflict, risk, communication, values, and other important matters, and consider how you should use these insights in your sales life, as well as your personal life.

The goal of this book is to help you acquire a new skill set—the ability to apply a knowledge of Personality Styles to your everyday interactions with each of these four different personality types. This is the foundation of relationship selling. It's understanding the perspective of the other person and prioritizing their needs to build a long-lasting and trusting relationship.

CHAPTER 1
ABOUT PERSONALITY AND PERSONALITY STYLES

Everyone is Different

Exactly what is personality? Psychologists tell us that the foundation of our personality is with us from birth. It is part of what makes us each unique. Oxford Dictionary defines personality as "the combination of characteristics or qualities that form an individual's distinctive character." However, personality is also influenced by all the experiences we have had. No one else has the same personality and no one else matches our exact perspective on life and how we respond to its events. Because of our personality and our life experiences, we each arrive at a different view of situations, and we respond differently to events and circumstances. You might think of your personality as your default system. It's how you view life. It's your perspective on the events that impact you daily. There are many personality models today, starting with Hippocrates' classifications and going up to Myers-Briggs in the 1950s.

While each of us is unique, we also share distinct similarities with others. To better understand personality, we categorize them into groupings called Personality Styles. Understanding the different Personality Styles provides us with insights into the differences and similarities in attitude, preferences, and behavior displayed by the people we encounter.

You might be wondering; *Can I deliberately influence my personality or Personality Style?* Here's my take on that important question: yes, you can by being aware of your actions and behaviors. When you consider personality when interacting with others, you will adjust your style to better interact with the other styles. If you are a "big picture" person and become aware that you're with a person who requires details, instead of becoming frustrated with all their questions, give that Personality Style what they are looking for. Some people are introverted, and others are extroverted. The breakdown is just about 50/50. Daniel Pink, who wrote *To Sell Is Human*, says extroverts sell a little more than introverts, but he mentions that ambiverts—people who exhibit qualities of both introverts and extroverts—sell 40 percent more than extroverts, since they adjust to the other person's personality.

Personality types are divided by how they tend to communicate differently, have different values and make decisions in different ways, and respond in different ways to risk, stress, conflict, and change, as well as by how they learn and teach in subtly different ways, choose different ways to relax, and have different preferences for their working environment.

Think for a minute about your own attitudes and preferences. How they are the same as those of some people you know, and yet quite different from others. Then let's look at the ten key categories that distinguish the styles.

1. Communication
Communication is the foundation of the selling profession and, frankly, life in general. Your communication skills help you get across your point of view, ask relevant and meaningful questions, and engage in thoughtful and interesting conversation. Yet, as I'm sure you have experienced, there are many styles of communications. As you learn more about each of the Four People Personality Styles, you'll learn the four distinctions in how people communicate, such as their level of directness, their enjoyment of small talk, and the level of emotion shared, to name a few. When you work as a sales leader, your communication with your salespeople is paramount. Understanding their styles will help you approach them in the manner they are most comfortable with. If they are direct, be direct with them and don't beat around the bush.

2. Values
Considering how personality reflects what each person values is critical to making sales and building winning teams. For example, is having lots of deep friendships the thing you aim for? Some people buy products and services solely to get the best deal, while others focus

WE ARE ALL DIFFERENT IN HOW WE

RELAX

RESPOND TO CHANGE

WHAT WE VALUE

MAKE

TEACH

RELAX

COMMUNICATE

WORK

LEARN

RESPOND TO CHANGE TEACH

DECISIONS

REACT TO CONFLICT

MANAGE STRESS

WORK

CALCULATE RISK

LEARN

TEACH

RESPOND TO CHANGE

WHAT WE VALUE

MANAGE STRESS

REACT TO CONFLICT

Communicate

REACT TO CONFLICT

LEARN

WORK

CALCULATE RISK

RELAX

RESPOND TO CHANGE

MANAGE STRESS

TEACH

MAKE DECISIONS

WORK

COMMUNICATE

CALCULATE RISK

RESPOND TO

CHANGE

RELAX

COMMUNICATE

MAKE DECISIONS

TEACH

WHAT WE VALUE

REACT TO CONFLICT

on the quality of the product. Some value great service, while others will place state-of-the-art technology above all else. Understanding what your salespeople value is important. Some will focus on winning at any cost, while others will focus on being the most technically astute with your products. Others will value the customer relationship first and foremost, and others will value product capability.

3. Decision-making

When your people make decisions in different ways, it can lead to contention. Some folks are impulsive when making decisions, others are very slow, and some are deliberate. Some need to analyze and make their decision based on logic, while others do it based on emotions and still others make decisions based on their gut feeling. Some consider all the data at hand and continue to ask questions to gather more information, while others are perfectly satisfied with the facts before them. When people on your team have a different approach to making decisions, it can frustrate those who don't understand why people decide the way they do.

4. Risk

Different personalities also view risk differently. Some are very cautious, while others are calculating, and another group will have no problem taking a risk knowing they can correct a mistake as they go along. When I play bridge with my friends from college, my friend Mike will be a little bit more conservative and hesitant in making a risky bid to game, while Joe has no problem shooting for the moon and going for the best score. It all has to do with their Personality Styles.

5. Conflict

People of different personality types vary in how they handle conflict. Some will retreat from conflict, afraid of friction and getting feelings hurt. Another style will attack conflict head on. Some view conflict as stimulating, more of a debate, and others are very concerned about damaging relationships. Maybe you just don't see why there is a conflict in the first place. Perhaps you don't know how to handle conflict and are totally frustrated by it. Many times, people view a situation as a conflict when in reality it's just having a robust discussion about why all parties have a difference of opinion. Some will get emotional, and others will remain calm.

6. Stress

Stress can adversely affect health, and how we deal with it has much to do with personality. Some will feel stress when taking on too much responsibility, and others stress out when there is little on their "to do" plate. Some will stress out when they lose control, while others just remain calm and think things will always work out. Some become more anxious with too much information, and others for lack of data. Some will bottle up their emotions and others will let them be known. Our dad was the calmest person my brother, Scott, and I have ever met. Every week when we called him, he would tell me and my brother this: "Remember boys, relax, don't worry, and don't knock yourself out." Our dad always was optimistic about everything in life and never stressed out.

7. Change

Each personality views change differently. Change can be invigorating and exciting or scary. For some it can be bothersome, for others inconvenient, and for some upsetting. Some like to keep things stable and predictable, and others enjoy the excitement and stimulus of the new. As a sales leader, being aware of who on your team embraces change versus who finds it frustrating will help you focus on those who need further explanation about why the change needs to occur. A good example of change in sales is when you reorganize your approach to the market. Some make changes based on a territorial approach and others by product type within the territory. The changes can be disruptive for some or not a problem for others.

8. Learning Style

When learning, some prefer a lecture environment with traditional testing, and others prefer experiential learning where you advance through trial and error. Some learn more effectively through hands-on activity, while others would rather read a manual. When I taught accounting at Dallas Christian College, I gave a real-life exercise to the students on how to run a business by asking them to select a business to run and then list what their expenses would be along with their projected revenue. We would then put the results into the income statement and balance sheet. Other professors would first review the concepts of the income and balance sheet, being more theoretical, where I would be more inclined to teach with active experimentation. Different Personality Styles have different strengths in their ability to learn.

9. Relaxation

Some people relax by having their alone time. Others prefer to be in the company of friends and family. Some people find competition relaxing, and others just want to read a book or watch a movie. When you take a vacation, some need to organize each day with scheduled events, while others like myself just take each day as it comes, enjoying the excitement of the moment and the spontaneity.

10. Environment

What kind of working environment is best for you? Some prefer to work alone, and others need the company of fellow employees because they need the daily interaction. Some seek a fast-paced environment and others enjoy one that is quiet and orderly. People are more task-oriented or relationship-oriented. Think about the type of job that attracts you. Some enjoy action and excitement, others intellectual stimulation, and some the satisfaction of achievement. Some need a job that demands neatness and order, while others flourish when they must handle the unexpected all the time and make spur-of-the-moment decisions.

Answers to these questions tell you a lot about your Personality Style. When you as a leader understand each of these and how your people behave, it will help you focus on what is most important from their perspective and adjust accordingly.

The Payoff—Why it's Worth Making the Effort to Understand Personality Styles

When you accurately identify someone's Personality Style, you will better understand how they view the world, how they perceive you, and how they will interpret your words and actions. This is true whether it's in a sales situation, a difficult team meeting, or in your everyday interactions with people.

Here are the four most valuable benefits of understanding the Personality Style of others with whom you engage:

1. Acceptance

It will help you communicate and connect with the other person in a more meaningful way. I have a very close friend, Todd, who is very direct and has no problem telling me what he thinks. Because I know his style, I take his responses in his context, and I never get defensive or irritated since I know where he's coming from.

2. Predictability

When you understand someone's personality, it brings your trust with that person to a higher level. As I mentioned, I love to play competitive bridge with my college buddies Joe and Mike. The most important aspect of bridge is sticking to your conventions, so your partner understands what message you are conveying in your bids. If I deviate from my conventions, my partner will lose trust in what I'm telling them. Personality is the same way. When I understand the other person's perspective, it will build the trust needed to work better together. Especially as a sales leader.

3. Expectations

The third benefit is being able to set the right expectations with your people. When I state that I'd like to see something done at a certain time, my salespeople know exactly when I mean. The result is a high-performing team, since there is no confusion about what we want to accomplish. I always tell my salespeople that they are the number one asset in the company. My most important goal is their success. When they're successful, I'm successful.

4. Other Focused

The fourth benefit is being what I call "other focused." When you consider and ask yourself what Personality Style you're dealing with, it makes for a more meaningful and productive session. I had one salesperson who continually asked me very detailed questions about our new product line. I'm a "big picture," highly trusting person. I needed to realize their style was being very detailed and skeptical. I needed to adjust my approach and be patient with their investigative questions and give them what they needed.

Why Knowing is Important

Knowing the Personality Style of a customer or prospect allows you to make an educated guess about which type of need may be more important to them. Is Mary more objective or subjective? Will John look for only the tangible benefits or the intangible ones also? Will their decisions focus more on the quantitative aspects or the qualitative?

My Personality Style—Orange—is known for making fast decisions that are more subjective than objective. When I decided to sell my car to my daughter Rachael, I then needed to shop for a new car. I really don't enjoy shopping for a car, but I thought I wanted an SUV, preferably one that was preowned and under $20,000. I was thinking about a Toyota or a Nissan. I drove the Nissan and it felt pretty good, and then I saw the QX 50 Infiniti. After two minutes of test driving it, I said, "Sold!" I didn't care about the price, the mileage, or anything else. I made my decision based on feel, which was quite subjective. I never buy something with a checklist of things I need. I base my decisions on feel and the intangibles. That's my style; that's how an Orange Personality does it! When you understand how your people make decisions, you can help them consider other options to improve their performance, knowing where their strengths lie.

The key is to tailor strategies specifically for each person's personality, using what you've learned about their style based on the list of categories above, beginning with communication and ending with environment.

CHAPTER 2
INTRODUCING THE FOUR PEOPLE PERSONALITY ASSESSMENT

After many years in sales, I grew more and more convinced that I was missing a big opportunity to make my approach to sales more effective. There was a gap in that many salespeople lacked an understanding of the personality factors that influence the course of the sales relationship and that affect buying decisions.

I am the sort of person who finds it easy to relate to others. At the same time, I am adept at establishing the objective needs of the customer and presenting the logically correct solution. Usually this helps me to bond, build a relationship, and move the sale toward a successful close. However, I found that sometimes this approach just did not work.

Why did my formula work in some cases and not at all in others?

On a sales call several years ago, I was engaging the client with small talk when I noticed him make an impatient grimace. I took this as a signal to get down to business. At that point, I asked the business questions I had planned and the answers I received were short and succinct—almost curt, from my perception.

As the conversation continued, they asked me very detailed questions about our services. I saw this as a test. My gut reaction was that he was trying to stump me, so I became defensive. I even became anxious because I was forming the opinion that they were not feeling at all positive about our offerings, our company—or me.

Today, I can see that my understanding of that sales-customer relationship was way off track. Let's dive back into that moment and see why.

As the seller, I had developed a perception of the client as challenging and skeptical. I stopped believing that we would win the business, and my behavior reflected this. Because I became defensive, every decision I made was made with doubt, not with confidence. It's hard to win when you're playing defense.

On another occasion, I was competing against IBM, and really thought I had won the deal. I was sure I had the better solution and the better value proposition, so I was disappointed when the customer chose IBM. I had focused on objective facts and logic, while the IBM salesperson had established a high-level personal relationship that gave the customer a lot of reassurance—a strong emotional pull in favor of the IBM solution. Again, emotions are more powerful in sales than logic, so never forget to address the emotional needs of your prospects and clients.

In the first example, I missed the mark because I focused too much on the relationship factors and misinterpreted the customer's need for hard facts as hostility. I assumed I was dealing with someone like myself, someone who viewed the world in much the same way as I did. In the second example, I focused on facts and completely missed the need for building a strong high-level relationship!

I soon realized I was projecting my own thought processes onto my perception of the customer. I needed to learn how to change my approach to include a real understanding of the Personality Style of the customer and adjust my own natural approach to match both the needs of the customer, as well as the nature of the solution.

To do this, I decided that there was a need for an easy-to-use, practical, yet accurate tool to help understand our daily interactions. After researching many of the personality tools, I developed my own color-coded Four People Personality Style Assessment, so anyone can apply the information in any business or personal setting. The tool uses four colors (Blue, Gold, Green, and Orange) as easy mnemonics for remembering personality groups.

What I was most interested in was developing a tool that sales leaders and salespeople would apply to their daily interactions with each other and customers. The questions are based on finding out how each Personality Style would go about communicating and making decisions, which is critical in sales.

When a tool is easy to understand and it's easy to identify and remember someone's Personality Style and the characteristics of each style, it helps us in building strong long-term relationships based on giving each Personality Style what they need. It also helps sales leaders to understand their salespeople's perspective and helps the salesperson put the needs of the customer first.

Why is This System So Effective?

First, with colors, it's easy to remember and identify the characteristics of each of the four Personality Styles. It's simple to add a color to the details we remember about the many people we meet, such as their face, name, and workplace, thereby remembering that person's Personality Style.

Throughout this book, the focus is not only on who you are but also who the other person is and how that person's personality affects behavior. We focus on how to apply the concepts to create effective communications with the other Personality Styles when you are:
- ✓ Selling products.
- ✓ Building and strengthening a versatile team.
- ✓ Leading and coaching your sales team.
- ✓ Being involved in personal situations and day-to-day business interactions.

Learning how to adjust your communications to achieve your objective is essential to connect with different personalities and understand what is important to them. The result is strong, long-term relationships with the people in your professional and personal circles.

Take Action Now

LEARN MORE

- ✓ Visit my website at ***www.StuSchlackman.com*** now to take the Four People Personality Style Assessment and discover your own profile.

- ✓ Check your characteristics against those described for your dominant style.

✓ Give the assessment to a few friends and compare their style against your experience with them. This will give you trust and familiarity with the Four People Personality Style system.

This will establish the foundation for the rest of the book, which will help you understand how to apply personality in your sales leadership strategies, including how to help your team interact more effectively with prospects, colleagues, and their family and friends.

Next Steps for Sales Leaders

Schedule think time on your calendar every week. Use it to consider these important issues:

✓ Begin a process to assess the level of trust on your team, determining what steps, if any, should be taken to build more.

✓ Find out how well you communicate with your team members.

✓ Observe how decisions are made on your team. Do you decide or is a consensus involved?

✓ How can you better leverage the strengths of the team to increase sales?

Focus on the needs of your salespeople as you understand what's most important to them. This will help you better customize your coaching to their individual needs.

✓ What do your team members value in their sales position and how can you better support them?

THE FOUR PEOPLE PERSONALITY ASSESSMENT

Taking the Assessment

SCAN ME

The first step in understanding yourself better is to take the assessment in the following pages if you haven't already. Or, if you prefer, you can visit my website, *StuSchlackman.com,* or take the on-line assessment on your phone with the QR Code here. Each has the same questions and will yield the same results.

Discovering the characteristics of your Personality Style is the first step in more deeply understanding your temperament. We all have all four styles or colors, but it's the order that makes you unique. That's what I call the sequence.

This assessment will identify your sequence. The questions cover the following ten categories:

- ✓ Decisions
- ✓ Relating to others
- ✓ Frustration
- ✓ Value at work
- ✓ Conflict
- ✓ Learning
- ✓ Communication
- ✓ Motivation
- ✓ Expression
- ✓ Making a purchase

Read each sentence and the four possible endings carefully. Compare each ending to the other three. Then determine which choice you think best describes you. **Put the choices in order.** Write a **4** beside the one that is most like you, a **3** beside the one that is next most like you, a **2** beside the one that is next, and a **1** beside the ending that is least like you. Repeat this step until all ten categories have been scored.

Most Like Me: 4 points

More Like Me: 3 points

Less Like Me: 2 points

Least Like Me: 1 point

You must be honest to make sure your results will be as accurate as possible. Don't answer the way you think you are or how other people think you should be. Don't answer the way you wish you were or would like to be—answer honestly, the way you really are. This assessment is geared toward your work environment, but also describes your behaviors outside of work. Each question is ranked so a number cannot be used twice.

Don't get too deep into the questions. Go by your first reaction to each question. It should take around ten minutes. When you're done, go to the Score Sheet that follows.

Good luck!

"DON'T ANSWER THE WAY **YOU THINK YOU ARE** OR HOW OTHER PEOPLE THINK **YOU SHOULD** BE. DON'T ANSWER THE WAY YOU **WISH** YOU WERE OR WOULD LIKE TO BE **ANSWER HONESTLY, THE WAY YOU REALLY ARE**"

START YOUR ASSESSMENT HERE

NOTE: If you've already taken the online version skip to page 27.

1. Decisions
I typically make decisions based on:

_____ A.   Research and analysis.

_____ B.   Practicality and my gut feeling.

_____ C.   A checklist and process to evaluate.

_____ D.   Trust and consensus.

2. Relating to Others
I relate best to people who are:

_____ B.   Energetic and upbeat.

_____ C.   Loyal and reliable.

_____ D.   Open and friendly.

_____ A.   Curious and knowledgeable.

3. Frustration
It bothers me when:

_____ A.   Others just ramble on for no reason.

_____ B.   There is too much unnecessary detail.

_____ C.   People are late and unprepared.

_____ D.   People are insincere.

4. Value at Work
As part of a team, I value:

_____ B.   Results and action.

_____ C.   Follow through and structure.

_____ D.   Harmony and cooperation.

_____ A.   Efficiency and ingenuity.

5. Conflict
When there is conflict, I tend to:

_____ A.   Address it with the facts unemotionally.

_____ B.   Get right to the point.

_____ C.   Approach it with preparation.

_____ D.   Avoid it if at all possible.

6. Learning
I learn best when:

_____ B.   I do things hands on by trial and error.

_____ C.   I use process and methods.

_____ D.   I'm interactive in a group setting.

_____ A.   I use discovery and experimentation.

7. Communication
I prefer communication that is:

_____ A.   Succinct and inquisitive.

_____ B.   Fast-paced with stories and analogies.

_____ C.   Direct and proper.

_____ D.   Sincere and open.

8. Motivation
I am motivated when I'm recognized for:

_____ B.   My performance and talent.

_____ C.   Planning and dependability.

_____ D.   My creativity and contributions.

_____ A.   My expertise and new ideas.

9. Expression
I express myself by being:

_____ A.   Calm and sometimes skeptical.

_____ B.   Animated and convincing.

_____ C.   Controlled and confident.

_____ D.   Pleasant and obliging.

10. Buying
I typically make a buying decision when:

_____ B.   I see immediate benefits and it's a good deal.

_____ C.   It's justified and meets a need.

_____ D.   It feels right and others agree.

_____ A.   I've done my research and it's the best choice.

Score and Sequence

To find your Personality Style sequence, go through each question adding the scores for each of the letters. In other words, add up the point value of all the A, B, C, and D choices you made. There are ten scores for each letter, and the total should be 100 when you add all the scores together.

Scores	Color		Color	Scores
D	Blue			1
A	Green			2
C	Gold			3
B	Orange			4

Put your highest score in the 1 column, then 2,3, and 4. Put the appropriate color in the box to the left. This is your Personality Style sequence.

1st Your dominant Personality Style   _____

2nd Your second style does influence you   _____

3rd Not much influence unless close to second score _____

4th Your lowest—least like you   _____

Your sequence tells you what you prefer most (your highest score) and what you dislike or care about the least (your lowest score). If all your scores are close, it means you can relate to each personality a little easier than when they are far apart. Having a high dominant score means you are stronger in the characteristics of that style, and if your lowest score is quite low, it's something you don't really care about and can be considered a weakness. No combination of scores and sequence is better than others. It's understanding who you are and how to leverage your strengths, as well as understand and minimize your weaknesses, that matters most.

Understanding the characteristics of your sequence is the beginning of understanding yourself and how you interact with the other colors/styles. As a sales leader, you'll better understand how to best work with your team and leverage the styles of each individual. It will greatly help you in coaching your team individuals and understanding what motivates them to action.

For the salesperson, you first must understand your own style before you can see how to better relate to your prospects and clients. Start with you, then focus on what's most important to them based on their style. Connecting better with those you encounter helps to build trust, a vital aspect of any relationship.

Visit my website at
StuSchlackman.com/Free-Cheatsheet-Download/
to view our in-depth offerings and support materials.

CHAPTER 4
THE BLUE PERSONALITY: THE RELATOR

The Blue personality type is the *relator* Personality Style. And before I go too deep, let me say that these are generalizations. Not every Blue Personality Style person will have all these traits. But notice how many of them seem to describe you to a T.

Let me introduce "Brad," the persona for the Blue personality, who is all about "people and passion." Their goal is to get along with others. In the Myers-Briggs model, they are like the intuitive feelers. They look for the deeper meaning in life. Understanding who they are and how they can make a difference is important to the Blue. Blues want to make an impact on society. They want to make contributions and they want to be recognized for them.

A good example of a Blue making an impact on society is my son Bryan. Back when he graduated college, he went on a trip to Europe with the goal of raising funds for water purification systems for Africa. Blues love to get involved in social causes. Bryan walked from Northern Ireland to Valencia, Spain, and was able to raise a significant amount of money while becoming a strong advocate for clean water.

Blues value honesty and trust. Blues will not make a commitment or a purchase if they do not feel the other person is sincere. They like to have small talk to get to know you on the personal side, not just the business. Maintaining eye contact with a Blue is important, since lacking the connection can cause suspicion.

Blues are good listeners and therefore tend to ask questions that are focused on getting to know who the other person truly is. For this, Blues easily open up and share emotions; they typically are transparent with others and look for the same in return. They are good communicators and are very aware of gestures and mannerisms.

Blues want everything to be in harmony and for teammates to get along. They dislike conflict and will usually avoid it. If Blues have been hurt in the past, their memory has a hard time letting go of it. It can seem like it happened just yesterday. When my brother Scott, whom you met in the Foreword, lived in France and had to close down a facility for Avon, he was distraught knowing that many people were going to be laid off. It bothered him for months after the building closed, as he thought about his team and the great relationships they'd built.

Relationships are what Blues value the most. Whether it's family, friends, or coworkers, they thrive on being with people and relating with them. Blues have lifelong friends and staying in touch and getting together for any occasion is what makes them thrive. One of my best friends in life, Mike Nader, is a Blue personality. Every time Mike has come to visit us, we received a thank-you card several days later. This is typical of the Blue personality. The thank-you card is not just a card saying thanks; it is a card that recaps the entire experience of being with us day to day and reminisces about what he thought was special. Mike is a true Blue. With Blues, if you don't stay in touch, they might think something is wrong. But for me, an Orange, it's not that I purposely don't stay in touch; it's that it's not at the top of my mind like it is for a Blue.

Blues are usually optimistic, and they are patient. It takes more than the other personalities to frustrate and upset a Blue. Blues are your steady personalities that can go along without making any drastic decisions or changes. In fact, Blues look at change as disruptive most of the time, since they like things consistent and predictable.

Blues are the most creative of the styles, since creativity is in their quadrant of the brain. We'll discuss more about how Personality Styles relate to the brain in a coming chapter. They thrive in a brainstorming type of situation. Since they have a creative flair, you'll find many Blue people working in the arts.

When it comes to making decisions, Blues take their time because making the right decision is important. It's based on feelings more so than logic; therefore, there is no rush. Also, a consensus is important to the Blue. If they are going to go out to purchase a car, it becomes a family event. A Blue would not make a purchase unless the family agreed with it. Also, if a salesperson is pushy with the Blue, the sales experience is over. Blues do not like to be pressured or forced into a decision. It has to happen in their timeframe.

When a Blue is in a sales career, their success is based on the relationships they develop. Their strength is in building trust, loyalty, and selling themselves first. For a customer, what impacts them the most about the Blue is their likeability factor and that they are responsive. Building strong relationships is the top priority. Since Blues are patient with customers, they tend to focus on pleasing the customer whenever possible.

Blues have a win-win attitude with customers and teammates. Making sure that everyone is satisfied is important. This is because of the empathy that Blues often have for others, especially those they are closest to. Blues will adapt to make sure others are pleased.

Blues also tend to avoid risk, particularly around others. Safety is an important factor for them. If the speed limit on a highway says sixty-five miles per hour, there is a strong chance that they will follow accordingly. They will also avoid risk when it comes to financial investments, as taking care of their family long term is of great importance.

When it comes to careers, Blues gravitate toward positions that are creative and those that require patience. Blues make excellent teachers for the elementary school years, since they are nurturing. They also do well in human resources, counseling, social work, nursing, insurance, real estate, advertising, and other areas that require high touch with people and relationships. Blues also do a lot of non-profit work and charity; they are keen to get involved in causes they are passionate about.

It is rare to have a Blue in a high-stress job. A job that requires numerous deadlines and conflict within other departments does not sit well with a Blue. What's important to a Blue when they join a company is their mission, vision, and values. Blues thrive in customer service positions, since they enjoy pleasing and satisfying the needs of others.

Blues enjoy getting positive reinforcement and feedback for a job well done. If this is lacking, they can become frustrated and disappointed. They want to make sure that their thoughts and ideas are recognized and supported by those around them. They thrive on being appreciated.

When Blues believe in something, they are all in. Whether it's a job, a cause, or a volunteer opportunity, what matters the most to the Blue is impacting the lives of those around them. They can become intense about what they believe in and can spend too much time accomplishing what matters most to them. The Blue needs to find the meaning in each of their endeavors.

The Blue personality is the glue of the team. Since harmony and cooperation are important, they will be proactive in making sure all is running smoothly on the team. If a new member joins the team, it is typically the Blues who will welcome them into the fold. You need Blues on your team.

Blue Personality Combinations

To better understand how Personality Styles intersect, let's look at these combinations and how they will affect you. Here are the three Blue combinations:

Blue/Orange

You care about the people and their needs. You come across warm and friendly and ask questions about the person. Trust is very important to you and you do not like to be rushed into decisions. You are very creative and can be artistic. When you communicate, you are very aware of body language and gestures to understand how the other person feels. You like people to get along and cooperate.

Blue/Green

You are open and friendly, and your strength is your passion for people. You are highly creative and intuitive. You make decisions slowly based more on how you feel than the facts. You like to express yourself and can talk about anything and everything. You need harmony in life, and it's very important for you to have a high level of trust in people. You enjoy your individuality and can go deep when it comes to idea generation.

Blue/Gold

You value your relationships and family above everything else. Safety and security are very important to you. The individual comes first and then the organization. You are open and friendly and excellent with communication and listening. You like to maintain order and make sure everyone is taken care of. You make decisions based on how you feel but will also look at the facts of the situation. You are strategic in your approach.

MY NAME IS BRAD AND I'M
A BLUE PERSONALITY

- What's most important to me is my relationships with friends, family and co-workers. I'm a people person. I value compassion, honesty and being open. I like harmony and affection.

- When I communicate I'm aware of body language and gestures and I listen well. I am figurative in how I speak and I love small talk about people and events. My strengths are my devotion, integrity and authenticity. I enjoy positions where I can be creative.

- I need to feel unique and I come across as authentic. I like it when people open up and express themselves. I enjoy quality time with loved ones, I compromise and cooperate and share emotions easily.

- I get uneasy when my feelings are ignored and there is conflict and confrontation.

- If you want to know how to identify me it's pretty easy. I'm warm and friendly and tend to focus on the relationship first. I will use words like caring, friendly, trust and family. I like to follow fashion and dress stylish with soft clean lines and muted colors.

- I unite the team.

CHAPTER 5
THE GOLD PERSONALITY: THE DIRECTOR

The Gold personality can be best described as a *director*. Let me introduce "Gloria," the persona for the Gold personality, who is all about getting it done. They are about process and planning. In Myers-Briggs they are known as sensory judgers. Golds value order, and one of their greatest strengths is their organization skills. Golds immediately take control to put things in the right order. They make rules to make sure everything functions orderly. They will turn chaos into clarity at all cost, and that's why they are the director.

On the other hand, since Golds are so structured, it can be hard for them to be flexible when a change happens that is not consistent with their plan, whether at home or at their job. This can be hard for a Gold personality in a leadership role, when they have to roll with the punches and deal with sudden changes.

Golds prioritize duty and service, and many times are driven to do things out of obligation—because it's the right thing to do. Golds commonly volunteer their time for service in areas such as watch patrols for their community, and other groups that service a city. My good friend Todd, who is a Gold, puts together the schedule for our watch patrol not because he was asked to, but because it must be done. The Gold will be the one to step up and be proactive.

Golds believe that everyone should be responsible. They are strong initiators of projects, activities, organizing, and getting things accomplished. Golds are more about giving than receiving, and that gives them a sense of self-worth. They believe in discipline, follow through and that everyone should do their share of the work.

Golds are very good with money. They understand its value and always evaluate whether something should be purchased or not.

There needs to be a reason to buy something, and a Gold will always measure the return on investment. They will evaluate the pros and cons before making any decision.

You can tell a Gold personality by looking at their bedroom closet. This gives you an excellent understanding of how they organize. Everything is always in its proper place. Shoes are organized. Shirts of the same style will be in the same section, as well as pants, suits, etc. In fact, all clothes will be facing in the same direction and even the hangers will be facing the same way. This is the opposite of me, the Orange personality; you might trip and fall in my closet. There is no organization.

The Gold personality sees things as predictable and consistent. There is always the right way to do things, and if it's not done right, it shouldn't be done at all. Golds get right to the point and are black or white on their opinions and views.

Golds can become compulsive about being orderly and following their routine. If things are messy, they will automatically start cleaning things up. We have one good friend who is a Gold, and you can tell just by taking a peek at her kitchen pantry. You know they're a Gold when their Campbell Soup cans are in alphabetical order!

Golds also desire punctuality and get frustrated when someone is late to a meeting. I conducted a seminar at Ebby Halliday, and one of the participants asked me when the seminar would be ending. He was a Gold and I told him we would be done at noon. Exactly at noon, he got up and left. The seminar ended three minutes later, but he couldn't wait. Golds expect you to meet your commitments and deadlines. I have another good friend I used to go jogging with. One time I was five minutes late, and he'd already starting jogging without me. I asked him why he didn't wait for me, and he said it was 5:30 p.m., which was our scheduled time to start. I just scratched my head, since as an Orange I was more interested in the time together than starting on time.

Not only do Golds schedule their lives, but they are fanatical about following their to-do list. At the end of the day, they feel good when they've achieved everything they set out to get done for the day.

If their schedule gets disrupted, it can be highly frustrating. When meetings are canceled or moved around, it can ruin their day, since they had in mind what they wanted to accomplish before the day even started. The reason for this is because Golds measure everything so they can feel good about their accomplishments. That's why the best project managers in companies are typically Golds. The mantra is "on time—on budget."

Golds believe in action steps and action plans. They believe in using Robert's Rules of Order for meetings. A meeting is a waste of time in their view if there is no agenda. Everyone needs to know the reason for the meeting and what will be accomplished. There must be action items from meetings and a clear decision about who will take ownership of them.

The rules in society are created by Golds. If they walk into a situation that is lacking clarity on who does what or what steps should be taken in a process, the Gold will take control and set the rules and expectations for the operation of that specific business process. Breaking or not following the rules is highly frustrating for the Gold personality.

Golds are excellent at planning for the future when it comes to investments, purchases, and taking care of their household. They are very good about saving for a rainy day and want to make sure all is protected just in case something goes wrong. They tend to be pessimistic due to their mindset of looking at what might go wrong, whereas I, as an optimistic Orange, don't even think something might go wrong—even more so since my lowest Personality Style is Gold.

Golds gravitate to clubs and organizations just to have a sense of belonging and because they feel it's the right thing to do. My good friend Glen, who is a Gold, was president of our high school class all three years and belonged to several groups that supported the student body. For Glen, it was the right thing to do.

As responsible people, Golds always put work before play. I wish I could say the same as an Orange, but if an opportunity to play golf comes along, I just might rearrange my schedule. Of course, as an

Orange I don't always have a schedule, so that's easy.

Golds are very predictable about getting things done when they're committed to a deadline. This is a top priority, as it has to do with their work ethic and making and keeping commitments. Breaking a commitment is unacceptable and unprofessional.

Golds are traditional, and as they get older, they become more set in their ways. You will see that Golds want holidays and traditions to go a certain way each year. Whether it's Thanksgiving, Christmas, or another event such as an anniversary, Golds put high value on family gatherings and other events.

Like Blues, Golds see change as disruptive most of the time. They like to see things running smoothly without any glitches. In other words, if it ain't broke, don't fix it.

You can rely on the Gold personality as an employee, since they are dedicated to their organization and its goals. They will get things done whether they have support or not. Golds will take the initiative when others are hesitant. They pride themselves in being responsible.

Golds rise in the areas of leadership and management. It's a natural progression for them, as they are interested in accomplishing the good of the organization and all involved. A majority of CEOs fall into the Gold personality. Golds do well in careers in education at the higher level, law, banking and investments, the military because it has rank, and administrative positions that need a high degree of organization skills.

Golds create the rules where Oranges typically break the rules. Golds ask for permission where Oranges ask for forgiveness. Golds enjoy being in charge and having control. This way they can navigate and define the order and rules that they think suit everyone the best.

When it comes to sales, Golds are best at selling the company where Blues sell themselves. They understand the benefits of their products and services. Gold customers want to do business with companies that are stable and have a successful track record. Stability, structure, organization, and order are what Golds value the most.

Golds bring consistency and stability to your team. They are the workhorses who make sure everyone is doing their share and that goals are getting accomplished. You need to have Golds on your team.

Gold Personality Combinations

To better understand your Personality Style, let's look at the combinations and how they will affect you. These describe the three Gold combinations:

Gold/Green

You need structure and process. Your greatest strength is your organization skills and planning. Again, you are very good at solving complicated problems and you follow a method to do so. You need to have an agenda for meetings, since you are orderly and structured. You are very dependable as well as loyal, confident, and direct. You tend to come across serious and listen well.

Gold/Blue

Your top priority is family and friends. You are very loyal and always concerned about the organization and the people. You are well organized and traditional by nature. Change can come across as disruptive, and you like things running smoothly. You like a routine; you like to follow a schedule. Following the rules and procedures is important to you for the good of the organization. You are good with finances and conservative on monetary decisions. You look for a sure thing.

Gold/Orange

You are driven by the bottom line and are a concrete thinker. You want to know the facts, timelines, and schedules for when things will get done. You need to understand expectations, and you don't like surprises when something is late or costs more than expected. You are driven to accomplish things and expect everyone to do their share of the work. You like to say what's on your mind and have no problem telling people what they need to do.

MY NAME IS GLORIA AND I'M
A GOLD PERSONALITY

- What's most important to me is dependability and organization. I am person that looks for structure, security and responsibilities. I like discipline and dedication.

- When I communicate I can come across aggressive and sometimes sound bossy. I like balanced conversations. In meetings I need to have an agenda with the expectations set. I focus on the task at hand. My strengths are my self-discipline, my stability and predictability.

- I like it when people follow through and do what they commit to. I enjoy structured activities and sports. I like it when others are direct and focused.

- I get frustrated when people are wishy washy and not sure of themselves. And if you waste my time and come to a meeting unprepared I will be very disappointed

- If you want to know how to identify me it's pretty easy. I'm direct and fairly serious. I will use words like reliable, dedicated and organized. I dress conservative and follow the dress code of the organization. I wear well-tailored clothing and very concerned with being well groomed.

- I am the stabilizer or the team.

CHAPTER 6
THE GREEN PERSONALITY: THE DETECTIVE

The Green personality is the *detective.* Let me introduce "Greg," the persona for the Green personality, who is all about research and developing new ideas. They are your analytical type, and they are all about perfection and precision. They are the "get it right" person. In Myers-Briggs, they are intuitive thinkers. For the Green, logic trumps emotion. Think of Sherlock Holmes or Spock in the old *Star Trek* series. They are always thinking of new ways to do things, problem solving, and asking, "Have you thought about doing it this way?"

As a leader, Greg the Green is great at helping his people solve problems and think strategically, but he struggles with getting to know them personally. All his discussions are work-related, and his people would like to get to know him better. It's easy for him to get all the details of his business to upper management, but his boss often reminds him to motivate his people to overachieve.

Greens love to learn. For them, knowledge is power. The more they learn, the better they feel. You don't have to tell a Green to read a book and learn something new; that's their natural wiring. They thrive on logic and reason, their natural strength.

A great example of this is my good friend Trevor Hayes. Several years ago, we went on one of our Dallas Ski Club trips to Aspen. Trevor was still new at skiing and thought his best method of improvement would be to purchase a book on skiing. This is quite typical for a Green and totally illogical for me, an Orange. What can a book teach? The book explained gravity and how to approach the slope. Trevor's saying was, "Gravity is my friend." Today he is an outstanding skier, and he always refers to the book.

Greens are lifetime learners. Just ask my good friend and pastor

Hank Lamb, who reads over eighty books a year and of course is a Green. Being the most competent at their trade is a priority. The greatest strength of a Green is their expertise. For the Green, the means is "performance" and the end result is "ability." They are driven to improve, and they will research and practice until they arrive at perfection.

Greens are extremely innovative. Look at a company like Apple or Google, where innovation is the focus. Most of the people at these companies are the Green personality. In fact, Google gives their employees a creativity day to go off and create new ideas or new projects to improve a product or a service. Greens love their freedom to just go off and do.

Greens like to tinker with things and experiment. If they are into something that is intriguing, they can do it for hours and hours. For the Green, work is more like a hobby. Experimentation is something that comes automatically. When a new software application comes out, the curiosity of Green makes them the first to learn it and use it. It's like my good friend Don Jones, who's a Green; he taught himself how to use PowerPoint many years ago. I was amazed at all the charts and graphics he was able to imbed in his slides. As an Orange, I just wanted to figure out how to add a new slide into the presentation. Greens don't need any help figuring things out.

Greens are not too keen on rules. Golds typically make the rules, and Greens question the rules. Rules, from the Green's perspective, restrict their freedom. If you ask them to figure something out, having a set of rules is not part of their thought process. The goal of the Green is perfection, and it will be done at all costs.

Many years ago, when I was working at Digital Equipment Corporation, we had an award ceremony at the end of the year called DEC 100 for making 100 percent of your annual budget. At the time, I was working for Don Jones, my longtime friend and mentor. Several years earlier, the award for DEC 100 was a four-day cruise to the Bahamas. As times got lean, it became a one-night stay in Fort Worth. Not too exciting if you lived in Dallas or Austin. The year after the event in Fort Worth, Don figured out how to get DEC 100 to be a four-day event in Martha's Vineyard. He figured if he combined a little training with the event, it would be justified. He pulled it off, and I couldn't believe it! Only a Green would figure that out.

You can identify someone who's Green just by listening to the many different things they know. They are constantly reading, learning, and watching educational videos while no one is looking. Greens are typically introverted and enjoy their alone time to re-energize and do their research.

Besides pushing to increase their knowledge, Greens will challenge others to do the same. They want others to observe, learn, and discover what they have learned. You can identify two Greens in a discussion when they go from one intellectual topic to another. It's like watching a game of ping-pong. They also love to debate each other, since Greens are also the biggest skeptics.

Because Greens thrive on information and love to learn, they are incredible at researching when looking to buy something. Typically, they will explore on the internet what they're looking to purchase, and by the time they get to the store, they know more about the product than the salesperson.

Green customers are your toughest. They ask many tough questions, come across skeptical, and you never know where you stand with them. Because they need so much information to come to a decision, they are slow at committing. They must have all the facts, statistics, and know what the competition offers. A salesperson can become highly frustrated unless they understand they are working with a Green personality. Never push the Green to closure or make them look ignorant. You will lose any chance of making a sale.

When it comes to communication with a Green, make your point. Stay away from small talk, since that gets in the way of the information they are looking for. Greens prefer succinct communication. Like my good friend Rick Huskisson says, "Skip the adjectives and just give me the nouns." Well said by a true Green personality.

The best way to understand the Green personality on a sales call is to be prepared with questions that get them to open up. Green like to play their cards close to the vest, not giving you any idea of where you might stand with them on moving the sale forward. It typically takes the longest to get a commitment from a Green.

Rarely will you see a Green get emotional. They are typically soft spoken, patient, and do not like to be the center of attention. They prefer the sidelines and get involved when they see a good intellectual discussion or debate forming.

Greens prefer their alone time, so when a party or gathering comes up, they don't usually get excited. At a gathering, they will seek out a close friend and might engage in a lengthy discussion that will occupy the time. They are not anti-social but prefer one-on-one time instead of a large crowd.

Since Greens are avid learners and enjoy detail, it's common for them to have a career in the sciences. Disciplines like information technology, science, engineering, medicine, and dentistry are naturals for a Green. Their eye for detail, research, and innovation makes the Green incredibly valuable to society. Just look at Steve Jobs with Apple or Bill Gates with Microsoft. They are excellent examples of the Green personality.

Greens are always envisioning the future and what could be. If there is a better way to do something, it will usually be the Green who figures it out.

You need to have a Green on your team. They will enlighten the other members to all kinds of possibilities.

Green Personality Combinations

To better understand your Personality Style, let's look at the combinations and how they will affect you. These describe the three Green combinations:

Green/Gold

You want details to understand the situation. You are great at solving problems and you enjoy methods and process. You are succinct in your communication and soft spoken. You're inquisitive and diligent and can be skeptical. You tend to ask a lot of questions and you need the facts. Your biggest strength is your expertise, and you're probably an avid reader.

Green/Blue

You are very intuitive and think in a futuristic way. You rely on facts and logic but also have a creative and innovative side. You are slow to bring things to closure and you do not like to be forced into a position or decision, since you need to analyze all the details. You're very inquisitive and curious. You need the details to move forward, as you are a deep thinker.

Green/Orange

You enjoy your freedom to do as you please. You don't like to be restricted to a schedule. You do like the details, but you also like to see the big picture. You are an expert in your field and want to get things done right. In communication, you are inquisitive, concise, and don't like redundancy. You like to get things done on your timeline. You focus on the future but also are concerned with the present time. You like change to make things better.

MY NAME IS GREG AND I'M
A GREEN PERSONALITY

- What's most important to me is precision, competence and expertise. I am person that looks for perfection, intelligence and logical answers to difficult questions. I like ingenuity and perfection. It's important that I am knowledgeable and love to solve difficult problems.

- When I communicate I can come across skeptical and can appear cool and distant. I dislike small talk and expect succinct and relevant conversations. I enjoy work that is analytical and creative like information technology and the sciences.

- I enjoy being surrounded by competent and independent workers. I like it when people are detailed, factual and patient.

- I get frustrated when people leave out the details and when they get excited or emotional. I expect others to be thorough and look at all the angles of a situation.

- If you want to know how to identify me it's pretty easy. I'm typically quiet and introverted. I'm calm and soft spoken and ask lots of questions to learn. I use words like accurate, detailed and logical. I dress functional and efficient and don't really care about fashion.

- I'm the innovator of the team.

CHAPTER 7
THE ORANGE PERSONALITY: THE ACTIVATOR

Describing the Orange Personality Style is easy, since I'm Orange. But let me introduce "Odyn," the persona for the Orange personality, who is all about being the *activator*. Where my brother Scott is Blue and is careful and deliberate in what he does, I just barrel forward. The Orange is the "get appreciated" type. In Myers-Briggs, they are sensory perceivers and have a great imagination. Oranges can have that "aha" moment where they connect the dots that a Green personality might have created.

As a leader, Odyn's challenge is to manage his time better and be more organized in giving his team members the direction they need. He's relational and excites his team members but must improve his follow-through on commitments.

One of the drawbacks of the Orange that I can easily admit to is that I don't have patience. Just watch me drive. I expect the highway to part like the Red Sea. Ask my wife Betty, who is my best witness. Oranges need momentum. They need to have things moving at a fast pace or they get bored. It's easy to lose the attention of an Orange if something is slow-moving, boring, or too detailed. Oranges are your "big picture" people. Just get to the point, help me understand what you're trying to accomplish, and let's get to it!

A great example is from my first job out of college. It's hard to believe that as an Orange I have a degree in Mechanical Engineering—I'll explain more about that later in the book. But my first job was taking off piping and fittings from a blueprint for nuclear power plants. My supervisor explained to me what was to be accomplished and then I went about doing the job. Two days later, I turned in the complete project. This made the entire department upset because I had two weeks to complete the project, but no one had told me that. Yes,

Oranges are fast paced because they get bored easily. They might start many different projects and not get them completed. Since I like to be recognized, I focus on getting the job done so I can get that pat on the back that I so much enjoy.

Impulsivity is in the Orange quadrant of the brain, which causes the impatience, boredom, and spur-of-the-moment decisions. Therefore, Oranges are risk takers; they find change exciting and like to multi-task. In fact, as I'm writing this, I've already taken several breaks this morning to delve into something else I needed to get done.

Oranges want action and they enjoy their freedom. As an engineer, early on I did not enjoy what I was doing. Sitting at a drawing board all day counting pipe fittings for the Extraction Steam system for a Pressurized Water Reactor was not my idea of excitement. Many Oranges will get into the world of sales, like I did later in life, because of the many different responsibilities in the sales environment. I might do some cold calling, prospecting, putting together a solution, present to a client, or try to gain commitment. That excites me. Especially working with customers. Oranges enjoy building relationships and are very good at connecting and networking.

One problem Oranges can have is doing too much of the talking. They love to be in the spotlight and be the center of attention. This can lead to smothering a conversation and not gaining enough information from the other person. Oranges think from their own perspective, which can be detrimental in a sales situation. Where my brother Scott, as a Blue, likes to learn about the other person and build a relationship, I will try to do the same and not realize that I might be hogging the conversation and completing the other person's sentences. That doesn't work.

Oranges get excited easily and are the most optimistic of the Personality Styles. This can lead to unrealistic expectations that might set them up for disappointment. Especially when it comes to my golf game. If my game is going well, I'll start thinking, if I par the next three holes, I can shoot in the low 80s. Then comes the high-risk shot under the tree and over the pond. Instead of laying up to set up an easy shot to the green, I'll take the risk of trying to get over the pond and onto the green. So much for being realistic and goodbye low 80s!

Another trait of the Orange is that the means is "ability" and the end result is "performance." That is the opposite of the Green style in the previous chapter. In other words, I don't like to practice. When I play tennis, there is no reason to practice my serve. Let's just start playing and I'll warm up as we play. It drives my wife Betty crazy.

Oranges live for the moment; it's the now that matters, and being spontaneous is my mode of operation. Where a Gold might plan each day on a vacation down to each detail, I don't even know the day we're flying out of town. Neither does my wife Betty, who is also an Orange. We've gone to a wedding on the wrong Saturday and have missed two flights because we showed up a day late. Not good.

Oranges also don't mind crises. Since we are highly competitive and look at everything in life as a game, we take crises as a challenge we need to conquer. Problem solving and getting things accomplished is more of a competitive challenge to me than a job. Oranges get excited when faced with a challenge. They also like to shine in the limelight. I asked one insurance sales agent why they enjoy selling, and his answer was that he likes to make a lot of money and be the hero to his family. That's exactly the Orange's mindset, and yes, Oranges do get excited about the opportunity to make big sales commissions. This can also be a drawback, as they might have the wrong focus for doing business, and yes, I have to keep myself in check on that.

Oranges are very hands on. As I mentioned, they are sensory perceivers in Myers-Briggs. They would rather do something than learn something from a book. In other words, show me how to do it. You will find many Oranges in trades such as carpentry, plumbing, electrical, and masonry. Doing a different job every couple of hours, getting into their truck, and going to the next different job fits the Orange Personality Style.

Since Oranges enjoy being the center of attention, you will experience hearing many stories from them and maybe even several jokes. Oranges enjoy entertaining others, making them laugh, and turning a possibly boring time into lots of fun. If they find a function boring, they will try to spice it up by taking the main stage.

Oranges have great stamina and in tough situations are typically the best at weathering the storm. They are resilient when it comes to tough times and facing possible defeat. This is primarily due to their optimism. They are the least of the Personality Styles to play the victim. Even though I can be serious, most of the time as an Orange, I'm light-hearted and jovial.

Oranges are typically the ones to take a challenge first or volunteer. They are bold in their approach and like to jump in headfirst. Oranges are not afraid to make a mistake, learn from it, correct mid-stream, and move on. It's better than planning and trying to do things to perfection. That is the mindset of the Orange.

Oranges usually are attracted to action jobs like sales and marketing. Also, a high percentage of professional speakers are Orange. They love being center stage and getting the attention from others. They love to please the crowd. Oranges make great entrepreneurs, since that don't have a problem with risk. High risk, high reward. Oranges make great fighter pilots like Tom Cruise in the movie *Top Gun*. They also are great at negotiating; to the Orange, it's a game and we must win.

Oranges want action, that's the bottom line. They are the energizer bunny of the team. They'll keep everyone motivated to press on and get the job done. You need an Orange on your team.

Orange Personality Combinations

To better understand your Personality Style, let's look at the combinations and how they will affect you. These describe the three Orange combinations:

Orange/Green

You are outgoing and friendly. You like change because you can get bored with the way things are. Performance is very important to you, and so is winning. You enjoy crises because you take them on as a challenge. You enjoy variety and are good at multi-tasking, since you can get bored staying focused on one thing for to long. You're persuasive and competitive and can enjoy a good debate. You like to tackle things head on.

Orange/Blue

You care about performance and winning. You look for immediate benefits and can be impulsive at times. You like to be the center of attention and love to be around people. You like your freedom, excitement, and have no problem taking risks. You are charismatic, energetic, and persuasive. You like things to move fast and get results. You like things simple and easy and will look for shortcuts to get things done.

Orange/Gold

You like to be the center of attention and prefer to do the talking instead of asking questions. You are action-oriented and a doer. Things need to get done and you move at a fast pace. You look at the big picture and focus on winning and the results. You are persuasive and bold, direct in your communication, and enjoy small talk. You will use stories and analogies to get your point across. You also need to know expectations and are bottom-line driven.

MY NAME IS ODYN AND I'M
AN ORANGE PERSONALITY

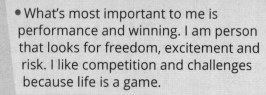

- What's most important to me is performance and winning. I am person that looks for freedom, excitement and risk. I like competition and challenges because life is a game.

- When I communicate I can come across bold, aggressive and fast-moving. I like to be the center of attention and like to get things done fast. I am charismatic and entertaining. My strengths are my enthusiasm, persuasiveness and skillfulness.

- I like it when people follow through and do what they have committed to.I enjoy working with people that are talented, skillful and energetic since I'm and optimist and love to win.

- I get frustrated when people are pessimistic, too detailed, rigid and slow. Things need to move along and get done.

- If you want to know how to identify me it's pretty easy. I enjoy talking with stories and analogies and tend to be outspoken. I enjoy small talk and use words like fast, easy, active and exciting. I dress trendy casual, like clothing with logos and tend to dress sporty to get noticed.

- I bring excitement to the team.

PERSONALITY STYLE RECAP

Here's a quick cheat sheet summarizing some of the key characteristics of each style.

Before we dig deeper into each of the Personality Styles, let's look at how each style shows up in leadership and what leaders need to consider as they build a high-performing sales team.

How to Identify Someone with **A BLUE PERSONALITY** Warm, Friendly, Sociable, Creative, Open **Their desk:** Pictures! Family, pets & friends **Their dress:** Casual, fashionable, soft/clean lines	How to Identify Someone with **A GOLD PERSONALITY** Formal, Structured, Factual, Controlled, Firm **Their desk:** Organized, neat, motivational signs **Their dress:** Tailored, conservative, formal
What to Expect When Meeting a Blue Likes small talk and want to get to know you. Listen, make eye contact & watch body language Want open and honest discussions	**What to Expect When Meeting a Gold** Values punctuality, direct discussions, agendas Likes to be in charge and lead the process Focused on expectations and solutions
What to Avoid Being inflexible with your solutions Applying pressure for next steps Ignoring their expressed feelings	**What to Avoid** Arriving late, and not being prepared Being too loose with facts and expectations Acting unprofessionally
How to Identify Someone with **A GREEN PERSONALITY** Curious, Detailed, Serious, Succinct, Calm **Their desk:** Devices, books, disorganized **Their dress:** Practical, comfortable, functional	How to Identify Someone with **AN ORANGE PERSONALITY** Excited, Bold, Competitive, Optimistic, Persuasive **Their desk:** Pictures with celebs, awards, trophies **Their dress:** Casual, sporty, eye-catching
What to Expect When Meeting a Green Open to possibilities that are relevant & objective Want details, facts and data they can analyze Expect time for questions and processing	**What to Expect When Meeting an Orange** Likes to look at the big picture Wants to get to the point, focusing on results Focused on success and achievements
What to Avoid Emotions and small talk Generalities; not enough details Expecting quick decisions	**What to Avoid** Being too serious Too many details Focusing on rules and regulations

How to Identify Someone with a

BLUE
PERSONALITY

Warm, Friendly, Open, Sociable, Creative

 THEIR DESK
Pictures! Family, pets & friends

 THEIR DRESS
Casual, fashionable, soft/clean lines

 WHAT TO EXPECT WHEN MEETING A BLUE
- Likes small talk and want to get to know you.
- Listen, make eye contact & watch body language
- Want open and honest discussions

❌ WHAT TO AVOID
- Being inflexible with your solutions
- Applying pressure for next steps
- Ignoring their expressed feelings

How to Identify Someone with a

GOLD
PERSONALITY

Formal, Factual, Firm, Controlled, Structured

THEIR DESK
Organized, neat, motivational signs

THEIR DRESS
Tailored, conservative, formal

WHAT TO EXPECT WHEN MEETING A GOLD
- Values punctuality, direct discussions, agendas
- Likes to be in charge and lead the process
- Focused on expectations and solutions

❌ WHAT TO AVOID
- Arriving late, and not being prepared
- Being too loose with facts and expectations
- Acting unprofessionally

How to Identify Someone with a
GREEN
PERSONALITY
Curious, Detailed, Serious, Succinct, Calm

 THEIR DESK
Devices, books, disorganized

 THEIR DRESS
Practical, comfortable, functional

 WHAT TO EXPECT WHEN MEETING A GREEN
- Open to possibilities that are relevant & objective
- Want details, facts and data they can analyze
- Expect time for questions and processing

✖ WHAT TO AVOID
- Emotions and small talk
- Generalities; not enough details
- Expecting quick decisions

How to Identify Someone with an
ORANGE
PERSONALITY
Excited, Optimistic, Bold, Competitive, Persuasive

THEIR DESK
Pictures with celebs, awards, trophies

THEIR DRESS
Casual, sporty, eye-catching

WHAT TO EXPECT WHEN MEETING AN ORANGE
- Likes to look at the big picture
- Wants to get to the point, focusing on results
- Focused on success and achievements

✖ WHAT TO AVOID
- Being too serious
- Too many details
- Focusing on rules and regulations

Next Steps for Sales Leaders

✓ Block time on your team calendar to have all members, including you and any support staff, take the Four People Personality Style Assessment and share their scores for each style with you. You can find it in an earlier chapter of this book or at

StuSchlackman.com/Personality-Assessment/Personality-Assessment.php

✓ Have them write a few sentences about their reaction to their results. What did they learn about themselves and how do they envision using the results?

✓ Schedule a sales team meeting where everyone can share their results from the assessment. Lead a discussion about how each team member can benefit from this information.

✓ Schedule ongoing training to discuss and reinforce the use of the Personality Styles in your team's day-to-day work. Bring real-world examples, then brainstorm how different styles might respond.

USING PERSONALITY STYLES FOR EFFECTIVE LEADERSHIP

Personality Styles in Sales

Understanding Personality Styles is important, especially for leaders. It is a powerful tool in the bag of tricks that every leader need to better connect with their employees and create results. Every team is a combination of Personality Styles, and each of those styles brings a different set of strengths and weaknesses.

The results of the Four People Assessment give you information that you can use to personalize your efforts to coach, mentor, and motivate your team.

DO THIS NOW

If you haven't done so already, start by having everyone on your team take the free assessment, which you found earlier in the book. You can also go to my website, **_StuSchlackman.com_** or snap this QR Code to take it.

When applied correctly, you and your team will certainly find the information helpful. In addition, you will be learning more about Personality Styles in a relatively friendly environment. This will prepare you well for applying the principles in your interactions with customers.

People from each of the four basic Personality Styles enter the sales profession. In our sales training workshops, we administer the assessment and then group the students into teams based on their dominant style. When we ask the teams in the workshop which personality is best in sales, everyone shouts out their Personality Style/color. In fact, each of the four styles can be effective in sales—but for entirely different reasons. It's not about *what* they do (they all sell for a living); it's about *why* they do it.

What drives each style to sell? Earlier you met Brad, our Blue personality leader. But let's think about him as a seller and see what we can learn. Brad is all about meeting clients and building strong, long-lasting relationships. He's best when you have a longer sales cycle. That's why I call him the *Relator*.

Gloria represents our Gold personality. For her, it's about the systematic, ordered process of selling and making recommendations. She takes pride in her company, typically leading with the strengths of the company. That's why she is the *Director*.

Greg, our Green personality, wants to solve the client's problems, digs deep with great questions, and enjoys coming up with the best possible solutions. He is the *Detective*.

For Odyn, the Orange personality, it's about winning and beating the competition, then building a lasting relationship with the client so he can keep on winning! The *Activator*.

Understanding the *why* behind your team's commitment to sales will help you help them. And don't forget to include all of the sales support people in your Four People Assessment strategy, training, and discussions.

Leadership and Personality Styles

We all know people who can be described as great leaders. But what are the key characteristics that make them great? As a voracious reader, I have read dozens if not hundreds of books on leadership. When I reflect on what I've read and learned, I've decided that these are the key qualities that make for great leaders, especially in sales. Here is my list:

✓ Excellent Communicator
✓ Confident
✓ Optimistic
✓ Empathetic
✓ Decisive
✓ Emotional Intelligence

✓ Engaging
✓ Shows Humility
✓ Possesses Integrity
✓ Strong Listener
✓ Servant Leadership
✓ Clear Vision

Now let's drill down on some of these qualities to better understand their meaning, look at how they show up in the sales environment, and their significance to leaders.

Empathy – Is the ability to understand your salespeople's perspective. It's being objective about what they're saying without judging them. Comprehending their emotions and the source of what is driving their concerns is important to understand, so you can communicate with them from their point of view. Even if you can't fix what the issue is, it's paramount that they know you care about what is concerning them. Working in sales is always a challenge and can be complicated with all the support organizations that work with sales and the customer base. There are many moving parts that don't always work in harmony.

Another frustration salespeople say is, "All my manager cares about are the numbers and they don't understand the challenges I face." I've seen this in many companies, and it ruins the sales team's morale to the point that every discussion has a negative tone. Trust goes out the window, and salespeople feel like upper management just doesn't understand the challenges they face. As a leader, you need to empathize with your salespeople. That's where you gain respect, and your team will strive to achieve the results you desire.

Humility – Is the opposite of pride. In my opinion, it's strength under control. It's having self-confidence and at the same time being modest. Someone with humility is humble. They are a servant leader who puts the needs of others first. Humility gains the respect of your salespeople, and they know you have their best interest at heart. A sales leader who shows humility knows that the credit goes to the sales team first. She is more concerned with the success of her people, knowing that the individuals' success adds up to the team's success. Obviously, if the team is successful, so is the leader. But too many times I've seen the sales leader take the credit or want to be in the spotlight.

Integrity – Is doing the right thing when no one is looking. It's having strong morals and ethics. The root word for integrity in Latin is *integer*, which is a "whole" number. Being whole is being upright and truthful, a characteristic every salesperson wants in their leader.

We hear the titles "sales leader" and "sales manager" all the time. You need to be both. Sales managers do things right. Sales leaders do the right things. They're different. Salespeople respect the leader when they tell the truth and know that the leader has their salespeople's backs and has the right priorities for the team.

Optimism – I believe those in the past who worked on my sales teams would say I was above average in this category. As an optimist (and too much of one at times, as with my golf shots predictions), you become contagious to the team members. Optimism spreads and builds momentum. P=MV. Momentum equals mass times velocity. As optimism spreads on the team, the results improve and the speed of execution of the team picks up. Optimism creates the enthusiasm that is needed in sales for success. If you are enthusiastic, it trickles down to the salespeople. It's believing in you, your company, and its products and services.

Customers want salespeople who are optimistic and enthusiastic, and that starts with the leader. Optimistic leaders encourage their people while asking them to stretch at the same time. They also shield any negative vibes that might be coming down from above. Your salespeople will go to battle for you because they believe in you and know they can win. Remember that sales is a competitive sport, and sales is about winning!

Decisiveness – Is about making the tough calls that might not be popular, but salespeople appreciate a great leader who makes decisions and owns up to them. I have seen many sales leaders who would delay deciding not because of the risk involved, but because they were afraid to look bad in the eyes of upper management. The goal is to decide based on what's right for your team and for the company. Making firm decisions in a timely manner and being willing to defend them is a direct indication of confidence. Every salesperson wants their leader to be confident. Decisiveness keeps the team moving forward in the right direction. Not every decision is perfect, but when decisions are made in a timely manner, you can correct them as you move forward if need be.

Excellent Communication – Having the ability to connect with your salespeople is paramount. Having one-on-one coaching calls is probably the top priority of every sales leader. Unfortunately, in the corporate world, the top sales producer is often promoted to sales leader and it's a disaster. I've seen it many times. How do you know if they have the qualities of a leader based on their sales performance? They are moving from being an individual contributor to a position where they are responsible for a group of people. It's a totally different skill set. You might be good at presenting and building relationships with customers, but selling products and services is quite different than leading and coaching salespeople. Coaching takes excellent communication with your people in the areas of asking the right questions, delivering constructive feedback when necessary, and challenging your people in a way that motivates them and doesn't demoralize them. Again, building trust with your sales team is critical to your success as a leader.

You can't be a great sales leader unless you have great communication skills. That starts with being a great listener, asking the right questions when coaching, evaluating their sales pipeline, and giving performance reviews. It's being open and flexible and giving your salespeople the quality time with you they need to improve their performance. It's being flexible and customizing your approach with each salesperson based on their experience, their needs, and yes, their Personality Style! As you will see coming up ahead, I will explain how to approach and coach each of the four styles.

Any personality type can be a leader, but different personalities lead in different ways. We need to understand each of the four leadership styles so the different team members know what to expect, and so team leaders themselves understand the impact their personality can have on other team members and team performance.

I'd like to share some insights from great leaders I've seen over the years. The best leaders establish trust with their team members, whether it's salespeople, customer service, marketing, etc. The best leaders view their people as an asset not an expense. In other words, they want to coach and invest in their people and respect what they bring to the team. They give autonomy to their people and trust them to do what's right for their business and for their company. Great leaders grow their assets. Treating people like an expense is always looking for what's wrong. That's demoralizing and will lead to increased sales turnover, which is the death of a sales team and detrimental to the company.

The best leaders understand their subordinates' Personality Styles and coach each individual accordingly. They coach every day, even if it's only for five minutes. They develop strong relationships with their people so they can challenge them and stretch them in a positive way. Great leaders help their people improve with direct and honest feedback that is taken by the salesperson in a positive manner without being defensive. The bottom line is great sales leaders are respected by their people.

Specific Styles & Leadership

As we look at each Personality Style in leadership, what might you expect from each style? Let me share some examples.

The Blue Leader – Brad, The Relator

Brad is a Blue Personality Style sales leader. His strength is his empathy. He's great at communicating, especially on a personal level, and knows his people well. Brad has built trust with his people. The problem is he has a hard time pushing back on upper management when he doesn't agree with something. He can probably exude more confidence with his people, since he puts relationships first and wants to be accepted by all. Since his second Personality Style is Green, he is quite intuitive when it comes to being strategic. He communicates well with his people but has a hard time giving constructive feedback. Brad is aware of his strengths and weaknesses and is always trying to put the interests of his people first.

Blue personalities are less common in a leadership position, preferring to facilitate. While they make excellent leaders because of their compassion for people, they care less for organizational skills and structure. The success of their people is more important than the goal of the team.

Leadership Abilities: Blues are good at reading people and understanding the strengths that the individuals will bring to the team. They are good at motivating others with their casual and communicative nature. Blue leaders have high integrity and put the needs of their people first. They are creative in crafting proposals and excellent at presentation development. Trust and integrity are great assets of Blue leaders. Their communication is open and genuine.

Leadership Style: Blues are open-minded and accommodating. They will lead by consensus and are always available for their people. They tend to be liked by all their subordinates. Blues are not into power and control, giving freedom to their workers. They are optimistic and encourage creativity and cooperation within the team.

Leadership Shortcomings: Blues don't like making tough and unpopular decisions. Blues have a hard time giving bad news to people. They will avoid conflict. Because of their nature, they can be slow or hesitant in making decisions, especially the difficult ones regarding poor-performing team members. This can lead to missed deadlines or results falling short.

Coaching Style: Blues are great at conversation and going deep with their people. They will typically start out with small talk and relax the salesperson. They are very trusting and will focus on the needs of the salesperson. They ask insightful questions but asking the demanding ones as it relates to performance can be a challenge. They are intuitive and will help the salesperson improve their skill set with strong insight. Blue leaders know their people well.

The Gold Leader – Gloria, The Director

Gloria is a Gold Personality Style sales leader. She's very organized and is always on top of the numbers for her team. she has consistent, well-structured coaching sessions with her people. She is confident in her approach to issues and decision-making and has no problem giving constructive feedback. Her people would like her to be more casual and not always so serious. Gloria is very tactical and can be a little bit more strategic. Since her second Personality Style is Orange, she can talk less and listen more to what her people have to say. She is aggressive and dominant in her approach and could lighten up a little. Even though she always has her people's back and tries to stretch her people to grow, paying a little bit more attention and finding more about their personal lives would build stronger relationships.

The Gold personality is a natural for a leadership role, and they are dedicated to the company. To them, the company comes first.

Leadership Abilities: Golds are very good at process and procedure. They are consistent, predictable, and very stable when in the role of the leader. They will not ask the unreasonable of their workers. Golds are well organized, predictable, and decisive. When it comes to the administrative part of sales management, the Gold personality shines. Forecasting and pipeline management are their strengths.

Leadership Style: Golds expect everyone to follow the sales process and follow the rules. Golds are goal-oriented and expect everyone to do their share. They set clear expectations with the team members. They require their teams to complete all tasks and insist on following up. Golds set schedules and agendas to manage everyone's activity. Meetings are orderly; they always include a reason for the meeting, an agenda, and a goal. With the Gold leader, you know where you stand on the team.

Leadership Shortcomings: Golds want constant updates on individual progress toward completing tasks, assignments, or projects. They can come across dictatorial, especially under pressure, and can be inflexible when it comes to company policies and procedures. Communication at times can be one way, where they are doing most of the talking. Golds do not put freethinking as a high priority.

Coaching Style: Golds coach more on performance results than anything else, and they will have a set procedure for a coaching session. They won't be any surprises and they have no problem telling it like it is. The coaching session will be balanced with an agenda. Golds will give their thoughts and opinions. What they look for is results. They will set follow-up meetings to check on progress. They respect those salespeople who are dedicated hard workers and will always be supportive for the salesperson's success.

The Green Leader – Greg, The Detective

Greg is a Green Personality Style sales leader. He's visionary and strategic and seems to predict what's coming down the road with his business and the changes in the industry. He's great at helping his people solve problems. When he coaches, he is excellent at getting to the key issues by asking the right questions. Sometimes he comes across like he's interrogating, but he's just trying to better understand what's going on. Greg's second style is Orange. That part of him can be more empathetic and open with his people, asking them more about what's going on in their personal lives. Sometimes he gets into too much analysis with the numbers and can procrastinate making decisions his people are looking for.

Greens are often visionary leaders. Bill Gates and Steve Jobs are good examples. Greens focus on future possibilities. They value expertise and knowledge as important qualities for team members.

Leadership Abilities: People will gladly follow a strong vision when it is well thought out. Greens love innovation. Greens like to streamline processes to be more efficient. They are constantly looking to make things better. They are great at solving complex problems and excellent at asking the right questions.

Leadership Style: Green leaders value competence and great ideas. Often, they play the role of the devil's advocate. Don't expect a lot of small talk from a Green leader. They will ask a lot of questions, taking longer to decide as they weigh all the information presented to them. They will also look at every possible alternative for proposals and running their business.

Leadership Shortcomings: Greens are not as motivating as a Blue or Orange personality. They also tend to rearrange information multiple times, which causes frustration for some team members. The Green can go into analysis-paralysis on data, which can cause indecisiveness. Being succinct communicators, Green can leave their salespeople questioning how they are doing and where they stand in progress in their job.

Coaching Style: Greens are more inquisitive than the other styles and therefore will dig deep in a coaching session. Their goal is to solve problems and help the salesperson to overcome any challenges they are having. Greens are succinct in their style, so there won't be much in the way of small talk. They will be innovative when it comes to helping on sales proposals, since they often think outside the box and are not sticklers for rules.

The Orange Leader – Odyn, The Activator

Odyn is an Orange Personality Style sales leader. He's great at rallying the troops behind him and helping the team hit their numbers. Odyn is not as consistent when it comes to his coaching, as he's very good at putting out fires on the spur of the moment. He knows his people very well and what's going on with them personally. Since his second style is Blue, he can get too close to his people personally and not deliver the tough news when necessary. He has plenty of confidence and loves to communicate with his salespeople. He can be more proactive about asking questions when he has coaching sessions.

Orange leaders are the energizers. They encourage, inspire, and have great endurance. They make the most optimistic, positive leaders.

Leadership Abilities: It's natural for Oranges to spur on the team and set a fast pace. If a crisis occurs, the Orange leader will jump right in to help fix it.

Leadership Style: The Orange leader won't sit around, so you typically won't find them behind a desk. They like to be in the trenches, engaged with a client, a partner, or a vendor. They are buddies with the troops and thrive on being around team members. Extra activities outside the office are a common practice. Their goal is to win.

Leadership Shortcomings: Paperwork, process, agendas, and a lot of meetings are bothersome for the action-oriented Orange leader. They will delegate what they consider non-exciting, boring tasks. The Orange leader might lack the details and can also be disorganized in prioritizing aspects of their business. They might not drill down with the tougher questions needed at times and can trust too easily. Hearing murmuring and complaining is not good for Orange ears. They also need to listen more and talk less with their people.

Coaching Style: Oranges coach to motivate and inspire. They will help their salespeople to stretch and exceed by encouragement. Oranges will ask what's going well and then will get into areas where improvement can be made. They do like to talk and having small talk on any topic is very common. The Orange leader needs to dig deeper with the right questions to help their people take their business to the next level and follow up regularly.

Building a Team

Building a winning team takes more than talent. The leader must have the right attitude, whatever his or her Personality Style. And the leader must bring together people who can work productively as a group to achieve the goals of the team, the organization, and the company.

A formula that I believe is valuable to any team is Trust = Speed/Cost. Stephen M.R. Covey came up with this formula in his book *The Speed of Trust.* He is the late Stephen Covey's son. When a team has high trust, the speed of their business execution goes up and the cost of the operation goes down. High-performance teams execute well when they have high trust.

An increase in tension within a team leads to a productivity decrease, while the opposite is true when the tension is alleviated. Again, this is built around high trust, strong communication, and understanding each other. That's where understanding personality gives your team insights into each team member's behavior, which then helps to drive increased performance.

Case Study: Cloud-Based Software Company with Annual Revenues of $65 million

I've had the privilege of training and coaching several large sales teams over the past decade with my friend and colleague Chuck Corbin, whom I've known for over thirty years. Chuck has been the Chief Revenue Officer for a cloud-based software company for the past several years in Frisco, Texas. What's interesting, at least to me, is that his personality profile is the same as mine. His four scores are the same. His profile, like mine, is Orange-Blue-Green-Gold with the same scores. The odds of that occurring are about ten million to one!

Chuck has done an outstanding job of building a winning organization with strong sales, professional services, client services, and marketing. He is fully aware of the importance of Personality Styles and understands how they have impacted his success in building a winning team. Being Orange backed by Blue, he motivates the team, communicates his intentions and direction, and motivates everyone to move forward. He is encouraging but at the same time makes the tough calls. Being low in the Green and Gold styles, he taps team members with those styles when they're needed. Chuck is well thought of by the entire organization because everyone knows he has their best interest at heart, and he values everyone who supports the organization's effort. In fact, he was recently promoted to CEO of the company and has led the company to increase its revenue by 100 percent.

Their Sales Development Team has been expanded from four to fifteen salespeople, which has dramatically increased the number of leads in their pipeline—the key to every sales team's success. Chuck realized that funneling more leads to the account executives to increase their weekly demos would significantly increase his revenue stream. He has used my Four People Assessment for several of his sales teams in the past. He knew that putting the right person in the right position would decrease the turnover and increase productivity. Typically, in the sales development role, turnover can be well over 50 percent on an annual basis, especially if you have team members with a Personality Style that has a hard time with rejection.

Chuck knew the type of salespeople he would need to build a successful team. The team is made up of mostly Gold and Orange Personality Styles, with just a couple of exceptions. While the Four People Assessment isn't an approved method for hiring, the results can provide you with such valuable information that you can easily match strengths with skills needed for various positions. We know that the Orange and Gold Personality Styles are better at handling rejection and are naturally more aggressive than the Blue and Green personalities. When Oranges and Golds interview and show interest in the outbound prospecting environment, we know they are truly interested in this type of position and have an excellent chance of success.

"PUTTING THE RIGHT PERSON IN THE RIGHT POSITION DECREASES TURNOVER AND INCREASES PRODUCTIVITY"

While Chuck is very successful, maybe his most important strength is that you will always know where you stand with him. His communication is direct, yet he listens well and considers everyone's input. His communication always ends with the question, "What can I do for you?" Chuck is a wonderful example of the benefits of having leaders who understand and utilize Personality Styles in their day-to-day business. Well done, Chuck, and as a friend of mine says, "Results rule." Success breeds more success, and it's a great thing to see.

This can happen in any sales organization when Personality Styles are considered in building and leading high-performance teams. It can make a huge difference when it comes to team interaction and team performance. In successful teams, the leader creates an environment in which team members interact smoothly and take on responsibility and accountability, and everyone is energized and motivated to achieve the team's goals. Understanding the Personality Styles of the team members helps the leader create that environment.

Knowing their own Personality Style, and those of their colleagues, allows each team member to adjust their behavior and accommodate the communications styles and needs of the other personality types.

Lastly, finding and agreeing to a certain Personality Style for the group allows all the members to fit into a clear group style: a "how" to complement the tasks of the group, their "what." A warning, though, is this: you should never hire someone based on a personality assessment. All it should do is indicate their potential success factors when it comes to the position, tasks, and environment. Every Personality Style has been successful in sales. When you know the style of your team members, you can coach them more effectively for success.

A personality-based approach should work for any team, whether it's a sales team, customer service team, an information technology-consulting team, or a football team. All kinds of teams can have their performance enhanced by understanding what strengths the members bring to the team.

It is also important to know what weaknesses exist and how to accommodate for them. Just imagine a team of all Blues, Golds,

Greens, or Oranges, and what those teams would be lacking! There would be no balance if everyone were the same. It would be difficult to harness skills and knowledge and turn this into results. They might not be able to handle conflict, or might be too structured, or lack creativity, or have no organization skills. Imagine a team in which everyone wants to work alone or where no one is allowed time alone to think and create. Imagine a team of all Oranges who want to delegate the details, but no one will accept what is being assigned to them!

Organize teams with people in positions suitable to their personality strengths while compensating for their weaknesses. This will maximize the team's performance, resulting in both efficiency and effectiveness.

Personality and Teamwork

Understanding the Personality Styles of your team members will bring teamwork and leadership to an increased level of performance. We begin to understand and accept why everyone behaves differently. We understand the unique characteristics of what motivates each personality, how they make decisions, how they view risk and conflict, and how they like to communicate. It adds a dimension of understanding that did not exist before. What once seemed like random inappropriate behavior is now understood as the interaction of different Personality Styles. It helps to understand why one individual behaves one way and another responds to a situation differently.

After understanding the differences, we must accept them. Only then can we make appropriate use of these different characteristics. Understanding which individuals have certain strengths helps us to know who will respond best in specific situations. In the end, it comes down to maximizing team performance by leveraging the unique talents of the team members. It strengthens the relationships between team members and their leaders.

Ivan Boyd was Chief Revenue Officer at GTESS Corporation based in Richardson, Texas. Ivan has been my close friend for nearly forty years. I had his sales team go through my Personality Styles workshop. When the team had quarterly meetings, the conversation always included comments along the lines of: "Of course Jim will get that done, he's an Orange," or, "Rick should look at that because he's Green." As a team, Jim and Rick closed the two largest deals in the history of the company by understanding their Personality Styles as well as the styles of the buying decision-makers.

✓ They tailored their team approach to the specifics needed to motivate the Personality Style of the client. So, knowing their customer contact was, say, a Green, they could reset their strategy to match.

✓ They switched roles, to lead or follow, based on whether the client would respond better to a Green or an Orange personality. This included building specific relationships with different members of the buying team, based on pairing each with their complementary personality match.

✓ Lastly, they reinforced each other as a team. For example, Jim, the Orange, didn't have to fear deep questions because Rick, the Green, was there to answer them.

Leveraging your team members' strengths will always improve your relationships with your clients.

At GTESS Corporation, account reviews of all customer contacts were categorized by their Personality Style. The corporation's service organization and IT group knew their Personality Styles; GTESS maximized team performance and relationships across all the company disciplines.

When we know an individual's Personality Style, we understand much more about the way they will respond to different people and their approach to problems, and then we are able to see how these approaches might differ from ours. The results and improvements in team performance can be extraordinary.

Now let's look at the characteristics of each of the personalities in a team setting.

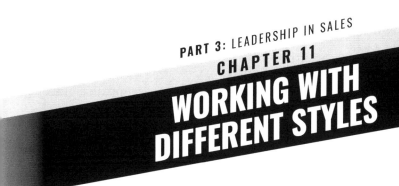

WORKING WITH DIFFERENT STYLES

Working with a Blue Team Member

Blues are interested in the well-being of the team. They promote cooperation and collaboration. They will be the first to welcome a new member to the team. For them, it's all about people and relationships. Blues are caring and honest with everyone on the team. They focus on the strengths of each team member.

Blues need to know that they are doing a good job. Giving them positive feedback is important to keep them motivated. They will build up and promote other team members. Blues encourage coworkers in their positions. They avoid confrontation and conflict and usually are slow to make decisions.

Blues will consider all the people involved when making a decision by examining each possibility and the possible outcomes. In a situation where there is potential change, a Blue will be cautious. They are not big risk-takers.

Blues are motivated by praise for their contributions. They like to be acknowledged for their creativity and their significance to the team. Blues enjoy the personal attention they receive from their leaders.

Working with a Gold Team Member

Gold personalities are strong at organization. They are usually the workhorse on the team and live by the clock. When work needs to be completed, a Gold is just the person to accomplish it—on time and on budget. They are good at watching the details and getting things right. Golds are reliable.

A Gold feels most at home in a structured environment. Golds do not want their time wasted. They want to know what to expect and expect an agenda with every meeting. Scheduling is important and so is timeliness. Sometimes Golds over-stress the importance of structure, at the expense of flexibility and creativity.

Gold personalities like to be in control. They are extremely dedicated to the cause of the company. Golds measure their worth to an organization by the work they get done. They expect everyone to work just as hard as they do. They can become frustrated if they are told to rush to completion a project that was not planned properly at the start. Golds view most change as disruptive and will question why a change needs to occur.

Golds are motivated when they are given public recognition and are appreciated for their dependability. They like to be rewarded with more responsibility and get energized when they are asked to be involved in the planning and organizing. They respect direct feedback on a regular basis.

Working with a Green Team Member

Greens are the best at solving problems. For the Green, work is play and they can go for hours on end till they solve a problem. Expect more questions from a Green than the other personalities. The Green personality wants to first understand the big picture before they dig deep into research and analysis. They will look at all the possibilities. They like challenges in work and look for innovative solutions.

Greens are more independent and enjoy working alone and without distractions. Most of the time, information is more intriguing to a Green than the relationships with people on the team. Understanding team members' emotions is not a priority to a Green. They will miss the clues that relationships are in trouble until a situation blows up in their faces; then they treat the event like a problem to be solved. Small talk can be a distraction to a Green.

Competency and knowledge are most valuable to Greens. Freedom is also important to them: allow them to explore and come up with new ideas. Expect debate and challenge on issues, since this is part of their nature. Sometimes bringing a project to completion is a weakness for a Green; often they will leave the details of the execution of what they created to others to complete. Greens can overdo debate and might over-analyze data, thereby slowing down decisions.

Greens are motivated when they are praised for their insight and out-of-the-box thinking. They enjoy being involved in decisions and love solving the tough problems. They are energized when others support their ideas and when they are encouraged to be visionary.

Working with an Orange Team Member

Oranges are the cheerleaders of the team; they like to spur the others on to win the sale and deliver the solution. Their mantra is like Nike, "Just do it!" An Orange's philosophy is to work hard and play hard. They are competitive; everything is about winning and looking good. Oranges thrive on risks and challenges. They prefer tangible problems, as they are concrete thinkers and are driven by the bottom line. Putting out fires is a pleasure for an Orange.

Oranges are usually the best at reading others and adapting a style that would be acceptable to them. Oranges will activate the team and keep the momentum up.

An Orange worker is often impatient. They prefer to get started on a project or task and not sit around and brainstorm or plan for long periods of time. They often multi-task, since they get bored working on one task for too long. Oranges like their independence. Speed and action are important to an Orange's environment; too many meetings are not a good thing, especially if they go on too long.

Oranges are more tactical than they are strategic. Their mindset is: "Just let us figure things out as we go along, and we'll get it done." Oranges like to delegate, and they look at the big picture. They'll leave the details to the others like the Greens and Golds. They are more interested in the results than the process to get there. Planning is not their strength, performance is.

Oranges are motivated when they are praised for their accomplishments and their performance is publicly recognized. They love tangible rewards like a trip to Las Vegas, and they love to be complimented for their skills. Immediate feedback feeds the Orange personality.

TEAMS THAT WORK AND WHEN THEY DON'T

Teams That Work

Winning teams all tend to have the following characteristics:

- ✓ Explicit trust between all the team members. The leader is just another team member, and everyone is a "wingman." Trust is more than honesty; it is knowledge that all their coworkers *will* perform.
- ✓ Explicit trust of the leader by the team, and vice versa.
- ✓ Open communication between the members and the leader.
- ✓ An environment that inspires new ideas.
- ✓ Members hold each other accountable while not being judgmental.
- ✓ A willingness to take risks.
- ✓ Responsibilities are defined and rewards follow performance.
- ✓ Members can influence the team with their thoughts and opinions.
- ✓ Mistakes are viewed as a learning experience.
- ✓ Each member is valued for their unique gifts and talents— their Personality Style.
- ✓ Members rely on each other—interdependence.
- ✓ Everyone knows the team's mission and vision.

When these attributes are present, the relationships between team members and leadership are taken to a new high. When the team clicks, the business results will follow.

Back in the mid-eighties, I was on a sales team that worked together and put the team's goals first. Often in sales, team members work as individuals to achieve their personal sales quota for the year. As an experiment, for one year we worked the budget goals for the good of the entire team. The team was as focused on the team goal

"SOLID RELATIONSHIPS BUILD MOMENTUM, LEADING TO STELLAR PERFORMANCES AND RESULTS"

as their individual goal. That year our team was number one in the country, achieving 286 percent of the budget!

Teams work best together when everyone has their eye on the same goal, whether it's a sales quota, a customer service metric, or a big game win. Team members must trust each other and support each other, to maximize and leverage the strengths of the team. When you have a winning team, you will see solid relationships that build momentum, leading to stellar performance and results.

Let's look at another example where extraordinary results happened because each team member valued the personality-driven contributions from the other team members. Years ago, a team brainstormed "how to resolve power lines falling when snow builds up on the lines in the Northwest." Brad, our Blue personality, noticed the meeting was getting tense. To ease tension, he jokingly expressed a wild idea based on his observations in his garden: "Birds fly past branches and clip the snow off with their wings—so, could they harness birds?" Odyn, our Orange personality, laughed, but knowing that anything goes in a brainstorming session, he turned to support this notion. At first there were general objections, but the Gold facilitator Gloria reminded the group: "There is no judgment on ideas while brainstorming."

Now, presented with a formal challenge, Greg, our Green personality, figured out that if helicopters could fly over the lines, the downdraft would knock off the snow. Having a workable answer, Gloria closed the meeting with assignments for getting it documented and carried out. A team can work most effectively together by having respect for everyone's ideas and contributions.

Why Conflict Arises in Teams

Conflict occurs naturally whenever people work together or live together. We know that everyone is different, yet it is still our natural tendency to view situations from our perspective and not that of the others. When conflict arises, it helps to understand others' Personality Styles, to minimize the amount and magnitude of disruptive emotional behavior. If we understand each other's styles, we can be more successful at improving our work environment and minimizing conflict.

Many teams shy away from conflict, but conflict exposes the possibilities that a team needs to explore. Conflict is a natural outcome of communication with two or more people. Conflict comes from team members having different priorities, values, and views. If we understand each of the four Personality Styles, we can better understand why conflict occurs, which can bring issues and problems to a quicker resolution.

Let's explore personalities in conflict on an imaginary customer service team. Our team contains all four personalities, whom you met earlier, led by Odyn. An emergency arises with a customer service problem. Let's visualize the dynamics of the team individuals and their different personalities.

The reaction: Odyn calls an immediate meeting of the entire team, to start in fifteen minutes. No pre-established agenda for the meeting exists. Everyone shows up to the meeting with their personal perceptions and needs.

Coming into the meeting: Gloria is upset that this meeting has disrupted her routine; she has a deadline for an assignment in two hours. Brad is worried about what the customer might think of the company, and whether the relationship will be at risk. Odyn wants it fixed immediately, and Greg want to know the cause.

During the meeting: Gloria wants to know the time schedule for the meeting. Odyn and the other Orange personalities want to get to the bottom line, go out, fix the problem, and get out of the meeting. Greg has plenty of questions on the root causes of the problem and how to alleviate them so that this doesn't happen again. Brad is concerned that the others in the room are getting irritated.

Conflict: The Blues and Greens want to spend the time needed to think through everything. The Oranges and Golds want to end the meeting and solve the problem. Oranges will just figure it out as they go with no details, and the Golds want a plan to follow.

Why? Blues value the customer relationship and team members

concerns; Gold's value the process; Greens value finding the cause and the solution; and Oranges value a quick fix.

This behavior occurs because Golds and Oranges are more aggressive than Blues and Greens. Golds and Oranges like to dominate the discussion, while Blues and Greens listen. Golds and Oranges tend to be goal-driven and are quick to decide, while Blues and Greens tend to avoid problems and move slower on decisions.

Another aspect of personality to consider is that the adjacent personalities typically have a more difficult time with each other. The Golds and Blues are in the lower left and right quadrants, and Greens and Oranges are in the upper left and right quadrants. Let me expand on this.

Golds can overpower the Blues with their dominant, aggressive, and direct style. The Blue thinks the Gold is not flexible enough and can cause conflict in their mind. Golds talk over Blues. Golds are serious while Blues are sociable and like small talk. Golds are decisive where Blues will wait on decisions. Blues have more patience than Golds.

Greens and Oranges collide when Greens want the detail and Oranges just want the big picture. Oranges decide on impulse while Greens can talk awhile and potentially get into analysis-paralysis over the details. Greens can sit and ponder, while Oranges want to get up and go. Again, Oranges lack the patience of a Gold, where Greens are more patient like Blues.

No matter your style, some behaviors will throw the different styles off-balance. Here are examples of behaviors that will irritate each style:
- ✓ For the Blue Personality Style—be insensitive or ignore their feelings.
- ✓ For the Gold Personality Style—interrupt them, talk over them, or be judgmental.
- ✓ For the Green Personality Style—be loud, bulldoze over them, or don't let them ask questions.
- ✓ For the Orange Personality Style—don't let them talk or ignore their presence.

If you are trying to build trust-based relationships, you'll want to avoid throwing your colleagues and team members off-balance.

We need to view the different Personality Styles as *different* and not *difficult.* Our views and attitudes toward each style are critical in getting along and leveraging our unique strengths. When we maximize our strengths, we minimize our weaknesses. Viewing each other as *different* (being open to opportunity) is a much better lens to have than *difficult* (being closed and inflexible).

This meeting is ripe for conflict and argument! However, when everyone is aware of their own and others' styles, they have a whole new perspective of how everyone would most likely respond to a situation, and better understand their behavior and approach. Team members can respect their differences by understanding what each member values and by understanding their unique perspectives.

OVERCOMING DIFFICULTIES WITH DIFFERENT STYLES

Different Personalities, Different Assumptions

Conflicts often emerge when there are differing views of **expectations, motives**, or **priorities.**

If **expectations** are not clearly spelled out then some team members will be surprised, upset, or disappointed by what is delivered by others. Each personality type has different expectations.

Different Personality Styles have different values; therefore, their **motives** can be different. A challenge that motivates a Gold team member might turn off an Orange—and vice versa—so having them work together on the same task might cause friction.

Priorities for getting work accomplished can also vary among personality types. What is the top priority for one team member might be the lowest priority for another. For example, an Orange will almost always set a tougher target for a project completion date than a Green. But the Green will always set a higher standard for acceptable quality than an Orange. The Green priority is for best quality while the Orange priority is for quickest completion.

Each style responds differently to pressure, deadlines, and control, having a different sense of urgency based on what they value. Oranges want to get it out and let it fly; Greens want to hold it close until it is right. Blues are cautious and don't want to disappoint, and Golds want completion and results on time.

If we can understand each other's expectations, motives, and priorities, we can avoid some conflicting situations. How? By being clear about what needs to be done and why, and by not assuming others have your same perspectives and views.

Let me give you an example. Are you:
- ✓ Serious or sociable?
- ✓ The type who prefers to dominate the conversation or listen?
- ✓ Detailed or more concerned with the big picture?
- ✓ Routine driven or someone who just goes with your gut?
- ✓ Task-focused or people-focused?
- ✓ Do it right or like Nike says, "Just Do It?"
- ✓ Direct or indirect when communicating?
- ✓ Reserved (introverted) or outgoing (extroverted)?

Most of the time you will see that Golds and Greens, being left-brained, tend to lean toward being serious, detailed, routine, task-focused, and the type who wants to "do it right."

Blues and Oranges, being right-brained, lean toward being sociable, more concerned with the big picture, preferring to go with their gut, people-focused, and "just do it."

Blues and Greens prefer to ask questions and are indirect communicators, while Golds and Oranges will dominate discussions and are direct communicators.

Oranges are typically extroverted while Greens are usually introverted. Blues and Golds are about fifty-fifty on the scale.

Irritating Behavior

Conflict can also result from personality characteristics that tend to irritate other people who have different Personality Styles. All four dominant Personality Styles have different values, communication styles, and approaches to work, and these differences can cause stress within relationships.

The following style characteristics can irritate the other personalities, leading to tension. Sometimes the irritation reaches a level that moves the tension up a level, into strife.

Blues can be too idealistic, too emotional, go too deep into topics with no closure, be too familiar or agreeable, and talk about too many personal issues. To other personality types, sometimes the Blue approach seems wildly off track.

Golds can be too inflexible, too controlling or bossy, too judgmental, call too many meetings, and get too bogged down on details. Sometimes their approach seems egotistical, power-hungry, or stifling to other styles.

Greens can be slow to make decisions, ask too many questions, and like to rework things to perfection. They question authority, give too deep an explanation, are too wordy, and too distant. Their approach often seems needlessly complicated to the other styles.

Oranges can be careless about details, impulsive, and impatient. They tend to ignore policy and procedure, they might ignore potential problems, and they're not great at planning ahead. Blues may find Oranges too competitive. Sometimes Greens feel Oranges jump the gun before the time is right.

When someone is behaving in an irritating way, we all have a natural inclination to assume that his or her behavior is purposeful and intentional; you think, *this is irritating me, so this person is doing it on purpose.* Yes, some personality characteristics can be wearisome and irritating for those with different Personality Styles. But ask around—other people might be quite happy with what is going on. Maybe it's you? (Or, more likely, maybe you both need to make some adjustments.)

If you understand the impact your natural personality-driven behavior can have on others, it will help you to temper your behavior and thus minimize irritation and stress in others. If you understand that the behavior of some people is so irritating because of personality differences (not just because the other person is being deliberately provocative), then, possibly, those weird behaviors will grow less weird and less irritating.

Handling Stress

Sometimes conflict arises simply from a stressful environment when the pressure is on, and everyone is tired. For example, when a hardworking team is tackling a complex project with tight timelines—and then the deadline is brought forward a few days. Or when a big proposal is due, everyone has been working around the clock, and then the customer changes the requirements specifications, but not the due date.

Some people will respond to a crisis by behaving unreasonably toward others, while others will withdraw into solitude. When fatigue sets in, introverts re-energize by being alone whereas extroverts re-energize around people.

Under situations of pressure, stress, and fatigue, the personality characteristics of everyone often become more accentuated. In the worst case:

Greens flood the team with information and ideas to get everyone to save time by just getting on and doing it the Green way.

Blues lose sight of the business objective and concentrate on the personal needs of themselves and others, even when some others would rather forget their personal needs and get the job done.

Oranges leap into action (any action will do) and expect everyone else to do the same. Plan? No time for that.

Golds become even more authoritative than usual, insist on sticking to the process (even if the process wasn't designed for the situation), and demand sacrifices.

Each personality will respond differently to issues that arise on the team. Conflict happens when these responses are markedly different or directly opposed to what other team members value.

Resolving Conflict

When you encounter a conflict situation, you should be aware that people behave most closely to their personality type when stressed.

This not only accentuates the disruptive aspects of their behavior, as described above, but provides us with some clues as to the best way to handle the conflict.

Resolving Conflict with Blues:
- ✓ Be pleasant,
- ✓ Empathize with their concerns,
- ✓ Don't be judgmental,
- ✓ Focus on the people aspects of the resolution.

Resolving Conflict with Golds:
- ✓ Define the issues,
- ✓ Don't criticize their position,
- ✓ Be responsible for your actions,
- ✓ Be respectful.

Resolving Conflict with Greens:
- ✓ Avoid emotion,
- ✓ Don't insult their intelligence,
- ✓ Focus on the facts,
- ✓ Encourage discussion and debate.

Resolving Conflict with Oranges:
- ✓ Don't take their challenge of you as personal,
- ✓ Be flexible,
- ✓ Be realistic,
- ✓ Offer alternatives.

The ability to prevent or resolve conflict is a critical skill learned by every successful leader and salesperson and by every winning team. Resolving conflict is healthy; done correctly, team and customer relationships can advance to greater productivity, greater resilience, and greater achievement. By understanding what each personality values, we gain a pathway to mitigating conflict, strengthening relationships, and building teams that achieve their goals.

Salespeople don't only deal with customers. They interact with others in their own company as a member of a team or a leader of one or more teams: an account team, a project team, or a professional services team. No one succeeds alone. We all need admin support, technical support, and someone else to bounce ideas off. Effective teams are basic to business success, including the success of sales teams and sales individuals.

If you want to build a winning sales team, everyone should learn about Personality Styles and receive training in the Four People Personality Style approach.

Next Steps for Sales Leaders

✓ Great sales leaders are:
  • Effective Communicators
  • Confident
  • Decisive
  • High in emotional intelligence
  • Engaging
  • People with humility
  • People with integrity
  • Good listeners
  • Servant leaders
  • Visionaries

On a scale of 1–5, rate yourself in these areas and then choose the three areas you will commit to working on over the next six months.

✓ When working with your salespeople, set expectations about how you will coach them and work with them. With Blue styles, be sensitive, patient, and build trust. With Gold styles, give them timelines, milestones, and follow through on your commitments. With Green styles, give them details and a rationale for your decisions. With Orange styles, give them the big picture, be action-oriented and set goals with timeframes for completion.

✓ As the sales leader, ask your salespeople where you can support them better to improve their sales performance. Base your approach on their Personality Styles to build strong relationships.

UNDERSTANDING YOUR OWN PERSONALITY STYLE

First, Know Yourself

Knowing yourself is the first step. Before you can extend this to knowing others, you must spend some time getting to know yourself. You should also observe the attitudes and behaviors of your friends and work associates and contrast them with your own attitudes and behavior. You now know what your style profile is.

Spend time examining your own strengths and aptitudes, so you can appreciate how they are linked to your Personality Style. Compare yourself to others. How are others different from you? In what ways are you the same as others?

It is also important to understand your weaknesses. It's much harder for a person to correct or improve a weakness than to improve a strength that comes naturally. Realize that your lowest style is most likely where your weakness is and what's least important to you. My lowest scoring style is Gold, a true indication that organization is a weakness for me. I have twelve to-do lists that all have the same items for me to do. One list I found was from six years ago with nothing checked off. Someone with a lowest score of Orange most likely is risk averse and not competitive. A lowest score of Blue might not empathize very well. A low score of Green might not be at all analytical or grasp technical points.

It's not easy for someone else to teach you about you. But the tools and approach of your personality profile can *help you learn* more about you. Take this opportunity—it will pay off.

From time to time, you may find it useful to go back and re-read the descriptions of each of the Personality Styles. As you become more familiar with the concepts of the styles, you will find that you gain more insights each time you refresh your knowledge. And if you are an Orange like me, you'll find it hard to do! But the more you understand about the different styles, the more accurately you will be able to apply the approach in your everyday life.

Me and My Style

You have already seen that my personality is embedded throughout this book. Understanding my Personality Style will help you understand what I'm saying as you read. Like you, I first had to discover my personality type to change my perceptions of others and my reactions to their behavior. So, what sequence am I?

When I created the survey based on the research, I discovered that my primary style is Orange. My other styles, in order, are: Blue, Green, and Gold.

I am in good company. Lots of salespeople are predominantly Orange. As a strong Orange personality (with a high Blue secondary), it is easy and natural for me to sit down with a customer and immediately begin small talk about sports, their family, current events, and so on. I can build sound relationships quickly as I am naturally outgoing and friendly. I am also highly competitive. Seems ideal for a salesperson, doesn't it? In many cases it is, but people like me can become better at sales when we know how to modify our approach to make people at the opposite end of the spectrum—in my case, Golds and Greens—just as comfortable as my Orange and Blue customers.

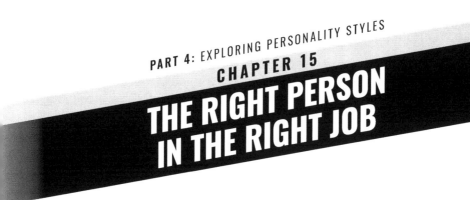

CHAPTER 15

THE RIGHT PERSON IN THE RIGHT JOB

A good way for you to become more familiar with different Personality Styles is to observe people in their working environment and understand what personality characteristics attract people to one job rather than another, what makes people happy at work rather than disgruntled, and how people gravitate to certain professions.

Don't Put an Orange Peg in a Green Hole

Any of the four Personality Styles can enter any field and be great at what they do. But different styles are naturally better equipped to excel in different types of job. Are you in a position today that is motivating you to do your best? What is it about your job that motivates you each and every day?

Some people go through life not enjoying a career because they were directed toward that career choice based on their exposed talents, rather than what their personality desires. If a student excelled in a specific academic subject, it was assumed that he or she should go into a profession related to that subject. Not always a good idea.

I was one of those people who initially ended up in the wrong job. I received my bachelor's degree in Mechanical Engineering from Rensselaer Polytechnic Institute in Troy, New York, and worked as an engineer for seven years before figuring out that I was miserable as an engineer. I finally moved into sales in 1983 and it changed my whole attitude about work. I finally enjoyed what I was doing.

In high school, I was near the top of my class in math scores. The school guidance counselor recommended I go into the field of engineering, since I was strong in math and science. Being a naïve seventeen-year-old, I thought, **Why not?** I was on the math team in high school and did fairly well, and I thought that going to a prestigious university would be great. Yet in my first year of college, I asked myself, "Why am I taking engineering?" I didn't really understand what it was all about, and I had no clue as to why I needed to be an expert with integrals and derivatives. What would I do with them? What are they used for?

I was flunking Calculus 1, not a good start to an engineering degree. That's like majoring in French and flunking French 1. I just didn't get it. As an Orange style, I am a concrete thinker and to me, analysis doesn't matter. What's important to me is synthesis, which is what do you do with the analysis. My good friend Elliot Goldberg, who majored in math, is a Green/Gold personality who knew his calculus. I asked him, "What do you do with calculus?" He explained it and I aced the next test with the highest grade in the class. An 88. With that I squeaked out a "D" for the semester. Now I know why I'm allergic to Excel spreadsheets!

Even though I had a 1.59 GPA for the first semester and went on probation, I kept going; I was not going to give up on this degree. Understanding now that I am an Orange personality gives me new perspective on why I excelled on the math team and completed my engineering degree, even though I was unhappy with it. Oranges don't quit and they hate to lose! We desire to be the best and win.

People with an Orange personality value competition, love to get attention, are bottom-line driven, and are concrete thinkers. I was naturally good with numbers, but my drive to excel in math was from my competitive nature to be the best, and not because I was fascinated by the elegance of logarithmic scales—as a Green might be. I wanted to be known in high school as the best in math and wanted everyone to know I was going to one of the best engineering schools in the country. Yet when I got to college, I nearly flunked out. Not exactly what you would expect from my performance in high school.

In retrospect, the reason for the meltdown is easy to see. My goal was **to get into a good school**, and once I achieved that goal, **the competition was over.** All I wanted from college was the degree, and there was no obvious reason to compete. Competition is what I value and what motivates me. No competition, no motivation—which equated to poor performance. I made it through my four years and received my degree, but as I look back, it was clear I should have been doing something more suited to my real temperament—such as tackling business school.

When I was in my engineering job, I sat at a desk for eight hours a day and analyzed blueprints—not exactly the type of work that stimulates an Orange personality! Oranges prefer action jobs that keep them moving around and having fun juggling different balls. Excitement and challenges motivate the Orange personality. I simply wasn't cut out to analyze blueprints all day. It took me seven years to figure that out. But that all changed when I moved into computer sales with Digital Equipment Corporation. There I had a great experience for sixteen years in sales, sales leadership, and sales training—all of which played to the strengths of my Orange Personality Style. I finally was in a career role that made good use of my temperament, working with people every day either training salespeople, coaching them as a sales leader, or visiting customers.

If we can understand someone's personality, we have a much better chance of understanding what they value and what will drive a person to deliver their best performance. This means understanding their full Personality Style profile and then putting this knowledge to use.

If my first boss had recognized my Orange/Blue style and understood the motivations and strengths of my personality, he would not have put me at a desk with the blueprints. He might have sent me into the field or into marketing where my competitive drives and respect for people's feelings would have aided the company. Or he might have tasked me with training the new recruits. If he was insightful, he would have moved me to a sales job.

Organization Personality Styles

Why do some people fit in just fine in a company, while others struggle to maintain their position? How is it that an individual can be mediocre in one company but can become a star when she moves to a different company, even when doing the same type of work?

Part of the answer is that not only do employees have personality, but so do companies. Companies have values, and when they become instilled in the way the company operates, they become part of the company culture. Company culture directs individual behaviors by peer examples and by directly, or indirectly, rewarding specific behaviors. This collective behavior can be said to be a "company personality."

Of course, we cannot administer this assessment to corporations. Nevertheless, we can look at corporate values and behaviors and compare them to the characteristics of each Personality Style. And frequently, we react to corporations as if they were individuals and expect actions and judge behaviors as if they were a person. Let me give you some examples, based on my experience, of companies with color-like personalities.

The companies I've worked for in the past had personalities that have either supported my own values as an Orange or made it difficult for me to perform. Their values were different than my own. Most companies have "mission statements" and "value statements" that state their intentions as to how they support their employees, customers, and the community. Some companies have an entrepreneurial spirit and take more risks than others. Some companies are very controlling, while others expect individuals at all levels to act independently to make things happen for the customer. Other companies are very process-oriented and structured; rules and procedures must be followed. There are companies that are technology-driven and perceive technology as their competitive edge. Yet other companies will put their employees first and value them as the company's most important asset. There also are companies that view employees as merely an expense.

If you are an Orange personality who struggles under the control of rules and process, you might be highly frustrated working for a company that has a Gold-ish personality. If you are a Green personality working for a company that is not technology-driven and doesn't put creativity and research as a priority in values, you are likely to experience disappointment.

One company that exhibits Blue characteristics by valuing their employees and customers is Southwest Airlines. The company, built by Herb Kelleher, is developed around their people and their trust in each other. Southwest empathizes and connects with their travelers. Let me give you an example.

This is what I heard on one of my flights on Southwest:

"Welcome aboard Southwest Flight 2122 to Phoenix. To operate your seatbelt, insert the metal tab into the buckle and pull tight. It works just like every other seatbelt, and if you don't know how to operate one, you probably shouldn't be out in public unsupervised. In the event of a sudden loss of cabin pressure, margarine cups will descend from the ceiling. Stop screaming, grab the mask, and pull it over your face. If you have a small child traveling with you, secure your mask before assisting with theirs. If you are traveling with more than one small child...pick your favorite."

Southwest thrives on fun and making each flight an enjoyable experience. Their emotional intelligence and personality set them apart from all the other airlines. In fact, they are the only major airline since 2000 that has not filed for bankruptcy. All they fly is the old 737, and you don't even get a seat assignment! But their connection with customers makes all the difference in the world.

If you are a Blue personality, you would love working for Southwest. If you are Gold, their environment might be too casual and free-wheeling for you, especially wearing their non-traditional uniforms. Southwest Airlines is in the customer service business and just happens to make their revenue by flying planes.

If you're a Gold personality, you might fit in very well with a nation-wide bank or a company like the old EDS (Electronic Data Systems) founded by Ross Perot. They are traditional, formal in nature, and have well-defined processes for running their company. Rules and process are important to Golds, where the outcome is stability and security.

If you are a Green personality, the research labs at Merck, Apple, or Hewlett-Packard might be a great fit. Creativity, research and development, and engineering are Green core competencies. As an

Orange, I had a blast working for Digital. Even though founder Ken Olsen, an engineer graduate of the prestigious M.I.T. in Cambridge, Massachusetts (a Green style, of course), did not believe in a commissioned sales force, we had the freedom to create and adapt to our customers' needs. Greens and Oranges work well in an environment that gives freedom to create and not restrict.

Nike is an example of an Orange company. The name "Nike" comes from the Greek goddess of victory. Competition and winning are characteristics of the Orange company personality. Nike's "Walk of Fame" at their headquarters has Joan Benoit, the winner of the Boston Marathon; John McEnroe, the tennis great; and Michael Jordan, one of the best basketball players ever. With Nike, it's about winning. That's why their slogan is: "Just Do It." As an Orange, I love that!

This is not to say that only Green Personality Styles will be happy working in a Green company, or Orange in an Orange company. Many roles exist in every corporation.

In the following chapters, you will learn, as a sales leader, how to best position each Personality Style. As employees, you will learn how to respond with understanding, and not just blind gut instincts, to the personality of a company. As a company, you can tailor your messages to each personality—not just your own dominant one. It is all about understanding and adjusting your perspective to address the needs of each personality. The strength of a great team is understanding and leveraging the strengths of all four Personality Styles to achieve versatility.

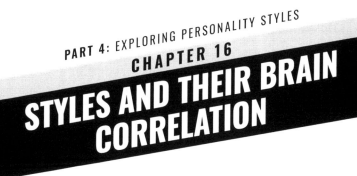

STYLES AND THEIR BRAIN CORRELATION

The Four Quadrants of the Brain

Learning how the brain is organized helps us understand the unique behaviors and views of each Personality Style. Left-brain people (Green and Gold) view information and situations differently than right-brain people (Orange and Blue). Greens, using the left front of the brain, focus on being rational and analytical. Golds, using the left back, focus on judgment and organization. The right-brain personalities, being more subjective, rely more on feelings. For Oranges, using the right front of the brain, focus on imagination and perception. For the Blue, using the right rear quadrant, feelings and emotions dominate their personality.

The left brain is verbal and hears *what is said*, the facts, while the right brain pays more attention to the non-verbal, which is *how it's said,* the feelings. The left brain is more serial or sequential in looking at events, while the right brain sees everything at once, making their approach more random, where they start from where they are most comfortable. The left brain understands the text, while the right brain understands the context. Left is about analysis and right is about synthesis. Left-brain people are more into detail and good at solving complicated problems with data, while the right brain is more perceptive and "big picture" oriented. The left brain is the logical side, and the right brain is the creative side. Remember, we all have both sides of the brain and a mix of all four brain quadrants. We're just more dominant on our main quadrant and side. The bottom line is that left brain styles are more objective, task-focused, and value the tangibles, while the right brain styles are more relationship-focused, subjective, and consider the intangibles.

As is common knowledge now, science has determined that men's brains and women's brains are wired somewhat differently. This is also reflected in Personality Styles. More women tend to fall into the Blue category than their male counterparts, and a higher percentage of men than women fall into the Green personality group. Women's brains are wired more for empathy and relationships, while men are wired more toward being task oriented. As an example, women shop and men buy. For women, it's an experience; for men, it's a task.

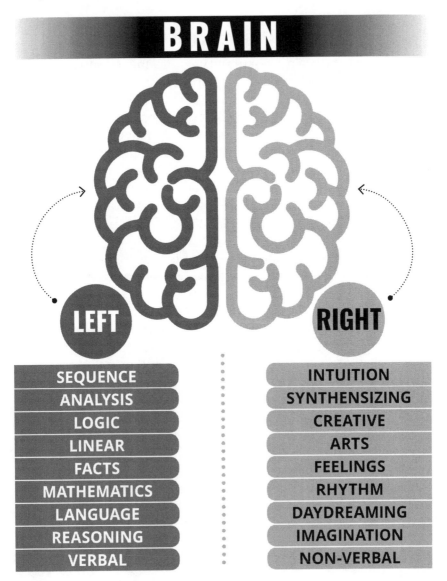

BRAIN

LEFT

SEQUENCE
ANALYSIS
LOGIC
LINEAR
FACTS
MATHEMATICS
LANGUAGE
REASONING
VERBAL

RIGHT

INTUITION
SYNTHENSIZING
CREATIVE
ARTS
FEELINGS
RHYTHM
DAYDREAMING
IMAGINATION
NON-VERBAL

The following chart demonstrates how the brain is segmented by the characteristics of each Personality Style.

GREEN	**ORANGE**
RATIONAL	IMAGINATIVE
ANALYTICAL	IMPULSIVE
CRITICAL	SYNTHESIS
NUMERICAL	SPECULATIVE
REALISTIC	PERCEPTIVE

GOLD	**BLUE**
ORGANIZED	SENSITIVE
TIMELY	EMOTIONAL
RELIABLE	CREATIVE
JUDGY	FEELINGS
PROTECTIVE	SUPPORTIVE

Does Personality Change?

A question that regularly comes up in our workshops is: "Does your personality change during your lifetime?" The answer to this is generally no, or at least not much. The relative order of styles in our personality profile stays the same throughout our entire life. What might change are the habits and views gained during the events we experience in our life. It can begin at home with our parents, immersed in the environment where we grew up. Did you grow up in a strict home or one that had few rules? Or did your parents give you lots of space to make your own mistakes?

I grew up in a strict home and had great respect for my parents (most of the time). You would have thought I was a Gold, never missing school and following all the rules. But when I left home for college, my Orange style was excited about my new freedom and I started to do the same stupid things most eighteen-year-olds going to college away from home would do.

Events that change our view and values can include getting married, having children, and getting a divorce. Our spiritual education also can modify our behavior and approach to life; and conversely, our fundamental Personality Style can influence our spiritual views of life.

What we do for our career will also temper habits we have, such as our reaction to timeliness and organizational skills. Let me again use myself as an example. Even though I'm an Orange personality, and Oranges are typically not punctual, I am never late for meetings. As I am in sales and sales training, it would be ludicrous for me to show up late to my own training event. Over the years, I have disciplined myself to be early; I have brought forward Gold characteristics from deeper in my personality profile, because this supports my primary driver to win at what I set out to do. Also, growing up with a dad who was never late certainly had a huge influence!

Another example might be a Greg, our Green, whose natural preference would be to work alone. However, if that person is, say, a technology trainer and is therefore required to work closely with people, he or she could pull attributes from her less prominent Blue personality, and as a result become generally more outgoing.

Blues, our Brad, thrive on sound relationships with people and do not seek conflict. But if a Blue becomes a trial lawyer, that experience will draw out his Orange characteristics. This will modify his attitude toward conflict and confrontation, and therefore his behavior.

Gloria, our Gold, who is very schedule-oriented and traditional, might learn different behaviors when placed in a context that requires impulsive action—for example, as a physician in an emergency room where rules might sometimes have to be broken to save lives.

Research has shown that as we get older, we increase our resistance to change. We do get comfortable in our routines, and disrupting them as we get into our fifties, sixties, and seventies often becomes increasingly uncomfortable. Where Greens and Oranges like change, Blues and Golds resist it. Now, we see everyone resisting the change in our later years.

Personality Styles and Culture

What about Personality Styles in different cultures? Tests have shown that the percentages of each Personality Style work out the same throughout the world. Every culture has every Personality Style in much the same proportions as do we in the U.S. However, other cultures, ours included, do develop stereotypes about foreign cultures. Stereotypes come from our perceptions—not from an objective test. So, if a person holds a strongly stereotypical view of another culture, it probably tells you more about that person than about that other culture. Different cultures might have strong characteristics like being punctual, being expressive, or even being relaxed versus formal.

Still, some cultures place great value on specific characteristics—which correspond with the characteristics of a Personality Style. Sometimes circumstances force a culture to act differently than its perceived primary style or acting like the perceived style could be inappropriate for the circumstances. In the case of culture, labeling by style is done to cast light on our perceptions, other people's internal cultural values, and how we should adjust to them. So, it is best done with caution and respect. Let's check if this makes sense.

From our American view, Brits, Asians, and Germans seem more Gold and Greener, while Hispanic, Latino, and African American people might appear more Blue and Orange. That is only a perception from our culture. Germans and Swiss, judging by the importance of train schedules, live by the clock, as Golds do; as a culture, they seemingly value and reward Gold characteristics. People from Mexico are seen as more relationship-oriented, so can be perceived more like a Blue. The English are formal and live by the calendar, so they are punctual but never too early. The French love to argue and converse and are labeled logical thinkers (after Descartes). But they are also seen as impassioned romantics (after their film style).

As an Orange from New York, when I moved to Alabama, I noticed a slower pace of living. Even though my Orange style friends in Birmingham had my same characteristics, they did move slower than me and were more patient at times due to the South not having the fast and hectic pace of New York City.

These stereotypes may be strongly held, but the reality is that the relative percentages of Blues, Greens, Golds, and Oranges is pretty much the same in Mexico as in Germany, England as in France, and Japan as in the USA.

Again, we view people through the influences of our own environment. If you visit Tuscany in Italy and you're from Texas, you might think Italy is the most beautiful place on the planet. If you're from Tuscany and visit Napa Valley, you might think that Napa is the most beautiful place you have ever seen. If you're from New York, like me, you've just got to love the spectacular West Texas scenery. (Just kidding!)

Our perspectives on what we value most, what we feel about our homes, and how we view other cultures are all very much influenced by our own cultures but are still consistent with our own underlying personality types. Just as our perspectives about our environment and our circumstances in life shape our views, our Personality Styles reflect our perspectives of place and culture. Different personalities have different perspectives. We are lucky to have these different views drawn from the four Personality Styles.

Are We Different at Work and Play?

Another question I'm often asked is: "Does my Personality Style change in personal situations versus business situations?" The answer is, generally, "No." We are always the same Personality Style.

However, the way we behave is influenced by the context. We might view relationships with people at work differently than relationships with family and friends. We might have a different attitude toward risk at work than in our personal life. The way we buy something for personal use might be different than the way we make a business purchase, perhaps exposing more personal tastes rather than emphasizing responsibility and accountability.

But overall, we find that our primary style displays certain characteristics that remain consistent in both our personal life and in business activity. As an Orange, I am competitive by nature. I value competition in my personal life the same way I do in my business. Blues value

"PERSPECTIVES ABOUT OUR ENVIRONMENT AND OUR CIRCUMSTANCES IN LIFE SHAPE OUR VIEWS, OUR PERSONALITY STYLES REFLECT OUR PERSPECTIVES OF PLACE AND CULTURE" relationships just as much in personal life and in business. Golds always value structure. Greens value knowledge and information in both personal and business situations.

But while the underlying preference stays the same, the way we express these preferences in our workplace behavior and social behavior can be quite different.

CHAPTER 17

UTILIZING PERSONALITY STYLES WITH OTHERS

Now that you have taken the assessment and know your Personality Style sequence, how can you use this knowledge to establish better communication and stronger relationships?

In order to gain a real appreciation of the variety of attitudes and behaviors encompassed by the Personality Style sequence, you can now appreciate the differences of the people you know well—work colleagues, friends, and family. Most people enjoy doing assessments like this and find the results interesting. The ten-question assessment has been designed to be straightforward to interpret and apply, and you will soon learn how it works.

As you become more aware of the four styles, you'll start to identify patterns in other people, and you'll become familiar with the behaviors that signify certain Personality Styles. You will increasingly be able to understand, and empathize with, the different attitudes toward *values* that underpin these different behaviors. What we value most establishes our motives for what we desire and how we behave.

Flip this around: *not* knowing someone else's Personality Style means we might not know what they value, and therefore, we will judge their behavior from our personality perspective, not from theirs. These kinds of misperceptions in our interactions can in turn alter their perceptions of us. In **Social Intelligence**, Daniel Goleman says "As we alter our perceptions, we can change our emotions." For many people, their perception is their only reality—in that they may not be questioning their viewpoint! You can now learn how to avoid this error and make it easier to identify with your customers and salespeople.

Back in Chapter 3, I described an incident from early in my career when I became defensive because I misinterpreted the customer's attitude. I thought I was being challenged when he was seeking information. This customer was a Green personality type. Knowing what I do today, if I had established up front that he was a Green, I would have approached the sales call with a clearer understanding of (a) what motivated the client and (b) how my own Personality Style affected my understanding of his behavior. Greens are inquisitive by nature and always ask tough questions. My client was reflecting his desire for information and detail, not questioning my knowledge. As an Orange, I saw interrogation, while he, as a Green, wanted an information resource.

Today, knowing that I am dealing with a Green client totally changes my perspective of the person as well as my behavior and approach. Knowing someone's personality will change your view of the situation too.

Greens are often not big on small talk, will ask lots of questions, are slower to make decisions, look for all the possible alternatives, and consider the future—exploring what opportunities might result from their solution. Now, whenever I identify a Green, I expect all of that and I respond accordingly.

I'd like to share a few more experiences that helped me to better understand Personality Styles.

My brother Scott called me on the phone and announced, "I've got Dad on the phone." Since Dad and Scott do not live in the same city, I jumped to the conclusion that if they were together on this call, there must be some type of emergency going on. Immediately, my heart rate was peaking, and I was ready to hop on a plane. I asked, "Is everything all right?" Then Scott reassured me, "Stu, everything is fine. I just loaded this new phone conference software program and thought I'd test it by conferencing us all together." As an Orange, my first reaction was to leap to the challenge—but there was no challenge. Instead, we had a pleasant conversation, the three of us talking about our kids, our golf game, and generally joking around.

Everything was going along nicely, but after five minutes, Dad abruptly said, "It's time to go," and he hung up! Had we said something to upset him?

Now, if you didn't know our dad's personality, you might think he was mad at us, but we know him well and realized he wasn't. Our dad's primary personality is Gold. Golds live a highly scheduled life. Knowing that, my brother suggested that according to his daily routine, it was time for Dad to get the mail!

Golds are like that. Several months earlier, my wife Betty and I visited my dad in Florida. We expected a prompt pickup from Dad but were left waiting at baggage claim. Why? It turned out that the reason we had to wait a little longer was because he had a scheduled dental appointment. Our flights were booked two months in advance, and you would think it would be easy to reschedule the dental appointment to pick us up on time, but that's not how Dad's personality is wired. Instead of getting annoyed at this, we understand that with a Gold, we just shouldn't expect him to change his schedule.

My other brother, Jay, was a Gold. From the age of twelve, each Saturday morning he would wake up at 8:00 a.m. and put together his schedule for the day as he ate his skim milk and Grape Nuts cereal. I, as an Orange, would wake up at eleven on a Saturday, grab a donut, and try not to get in trouble by 3:00 pm!

Golds are extremely organized. You can see this in their bedroom closet where all the shirts are in order by color; shoes are perfectly in a row; pants and suits are segregated by season. I have one Gold friend who alphabetizes his soups in the pantry.

What a Speed Limit of 70 mph Means to Each Personality Style:

✓ A Gold will say it's the law and you should go 70.
✓ An Orange will say speed limits are merely a suggestion.
✓ A Green will automatically add in an overage allowance and then drive at 73 expecting no risk of a ticket.
✓ To a Blue, it means stay close to 70, because otherwise you'll upset someone and get in trouble.

Trying to view situations from other people's perspective is the first step in understanding why each personality behaves differently. We start to understand their priorities and motivations. We build an appreciation of why people do things, not just what they do.

Use with Care and Consideration

There are some rules we need to understand when we start using Personality Styles. Here are five of the most important:

1. Don't stereotype people based on their dominant Personality Style. Not all Blues are the same, and this is true for the other three styles too. Everyone is unique in ways that even their full personality sequence cannot completely capture and classify. However, the dominant Personality Style will have certain characteristics that they all have in common.

Let's look at an example of this. My primary style is Orange and my secondary is Blue. My wife Betty is also Orange, but her second style is Gold. Even though we have a lot of the same characteristics, sharing Orange as our dominant style, we also have differences. As indicated by my second style being Blue, I am more right-brained than my wife and generally more sensitive to others' feelings. I don't handle conflict as well as Betty. With Gold as her second style, Betty is more structured; she worked at AT&T for thirty-three years. We find that Golds value loyalty and also give their loyalty, which is fortunate for me. Betty's lowest ranked style is Blue; her favorite saying at work is "cry a river, build a bridge, and get over it." She doesn't get her feelings hurt as much as others. I guess that's good for me when I mess up. But this quote is not exactly something a Blue personality would like to hear!

The danger of stereotyping is that by assuming someone conforms exactly to the textbook description of their dominant style, you can miss important aspects of their true personality.

2. Don't try to change people. Understand their personality's perspective and give them what's important to them. Trying to change someone from their style and default will end with resistance and no one wins.

"BY STEREOTYPING, YOU CAN MISS IMPORTANT ASPECTS OF A PERSON'S TRUE PERSONALITY"

3. Don't negate the value of others. People naturally give more weight to their own strengths, and when they see these strengths displayed by others, they understand their importance, since those capabilities are directly related to what they themselves value and what motivates them to perform. However, this means that sometimes people can undervalue or negate the value that other personalities bring. Just because it's something we aren't good at or don't enjoy doesn't mean that it doesn't have value.

We should never negate the value that other Personality Styles bring to a team or a project. There is measurable strength in diversity and multiple perspectives.

4. Don't overdo a strength; it might become a liability. We tend to overdo it with things we are naturally good at. Even though Golds are good at organization and structure, we don't want to emphasize this so much that we miss out on creative ideas that produce positive change. Being too structured might end in being inflexible. Greens are always able to come up with new ideas. But there comes a point when the new ideas have to stop and implementation starts, not always a Green strength.

5. Do appreciate the strengths of each style. When you've assessed the Personality Style of someone, it's tempting to assume that they fit all the characteristics of that style. However, sometimes people don't exactly fit the pattern because we're all different according to our profile scores, where we grew up, and how we were raised. Therefore, before you decide on an assumed strength (or preference or attitude), test it out first. You should always confirm your supposition before you put it into action.

PUTTING THIS INTO PRACTICE

In the last chapter, I concluded by pointing out that if you understand someone's personality it will help you understand **why** they are doing what they are doing. How to work as a team, handle stress and conflict, etc. But how do you assess their personality type?

Early on in a customer relationship, it is hardly ever practical or appropriate to sit a customer down and ask them to take the Four People Personality Assessment. No matter how enthusiastic you are about the assessment, don't just walk up to a customer and give them the test!

When you know a customer well, giving the assessment to your customer's decision team is a great relationship builder, giving value to you and your customer for very little cost and time. But we have found that this is best done during a planned meeting after you have already developed a sound relationship.

Without the assessment, however, it is not always easy to accurately identify someone's Personality Style. So, do we have a Catch-22? You need to have established a good relationship in order to sit a client down for the ten-question survey; however, to build that degree of familiarity in the relationship, it would help to have an idea of their style.

Fortunately, there are some ways in which we can gain clues and insights that allow us to gather sufficient information to make a confident assessment of someone's dominant Personality Style, and perhaps even the secondary too. The beauty of the assessment is that it is easier than other systems to obtain a good approximation of someone's personality type through observation and discussion. However, it still requires careful thought and discipline to get it right. For an accurate assessment of an individual, he or she must complete the survey.

You can access the survey at ***StuSchlackman.com,*** with the QR Code at left or you can take the assessment in the beginning of this book (PAGE 22).

How do you narrow it down fast? Blue, Gold, Green, or Orange? With experience, this will become as natural as remembering someone's name. But for beginners, this is the most difficult task in applying the Four People Personality Style system. Here are some tips to help you quickly identify someone's Personality Style.

What Are the Odds?

This is a lot like playing poker—homework is important. You need to learn the character of the game before you can use it and learn the odds to judge your strategy. It turns out that Personality Styles are not evenly spread across the population. It's generally accepted that certain styles are more common than others. When we're talking about the four colors, the order of the most common style you'll come across is: Gold, then Orange, then Blue, then Green.

When you meet a random person on the street, it is two times more likely that you are talking to an Orange than a Blue. Three out of four people you meet will be either Orange or Gold. One in seven will be Blue. And only one in eight will be Green.

Most of the time, you will be meeting Gold and Orange personalities because they make up most of the population. However, because of their specific likes, each style will gravitate to specific activities. So, while meeting a Blue or Green in a random group of five is unlikely, the odds will increase if you are at meetings or places associated with their interests. When you find a Green, the probability of finding another Green in that setting goes up dramatically.

The location, environment, or activity where you meet someone will change the odds of finding certain styles. In the executive suite, it's more likely they are Gold. In the development or engineering organization, it is likely they are a Green. Human resources and marketing would lean toward Blue. In sales and among those who speak for a living, Oranges are likely to dominate the crowd.

Ask and Listen

When you're interacting with customers, try to get into the habit of looking for clues to help you identify their Personality Style. It is important to consistently keep in the forefront of your mind: *What Personality Style am I dealing with right now?* The more you do this, the more accurate you will become in your assessment of their Personality Style, and the more practiced you'll become in listening and focusing on the customer.

Try to extend the conversation and listen to both what they have to say and *how they say it.* Listen for not only **what** is said (facts and information) but **how** it is said (feelings and attitudes).

Every salesperson knows to ask the customer the basic question: "What are you trying to accomplish?" However, in the quest for personality clues, you must widen the conversation to cover areas such as:

"What is most important to you?"

"What do you see as your greatest challenge and your top priorities?"

"What would your approach be?"

The idea is to guide the conversation around these topics in a way that is relevant to the business you are discussing.

There are many more questions that you might ask. Remember to listen to their answers and take guidance from the clues communicated by the customer. When openings occur, probe deeper into their challenges and their view of their situation. We can more easily influence each sale if we understand our customer's personality and their perspectives.

As you process the responses, you can use your understanding of the left brain and right brain differences, described earlier, to start to narrow down the options.

For example:

Gold and Green personalities (left brain dominant) generally ask for facts and focus the conversation on practicalities—for example, details of the solution's technology and implementation process. They look for the tangible facts and are more objective. Return on investment is important as well as the details of the solution.

Orange and Blue personalities (right-brain dominant) will tend to talk more about perceptions and feelings, such as the impact a solution will have on their customers and employees. They are more subjective and will focus on the intangibles. Service and support are priorities for them.

Asking questions in these general areas helps to reveal a customer's dominant Personality Style. As you grow to understand your customer more, you will be able to use the more detailed style descriptions provided in Part 2 of this book to focus in on their dominant style, and in some cases even identify their secondary style.

Until you know which personality you are dealing with, it is smart to mostly ask questions and listen to answers, rather than express your own views. Let's look at some typical personality-related responses for each of these questions.

"What is most important to you?"

The idea of asking questions around the topic of "what is important" is to start to build a picture of what your customer *values*.

If the answer seems to focus around people (impact, feelings, perceptions) you may be talking with a Blue, the *Relator*.

If the response focuses mostly on financial aspects of the solution, ROI, and the impact on the company's bottom line, your customer is likely a Gold, the *Director*.

If you receive many questions about the technology, details of the functionality, and its future impact on the company's direction, that suggests you are dealing with a Green, the *Detective.*

"UNTIL YOU KNOW
WHICH PERSONALITY
THEY ARE,
ASK MORE
QUESTIONS
AND
LISTEN TO
ANSWERS,
RATHER THAN
EXPRESS YOUR
OWN VIEWS"

If the emphasis is on competitive advantage, gaining market share, and personal career benefits, the customer might be an Orange, the *Activator.*

"Your greatest challenges and top priorities?"

This is another good question that can help bring out values, and areas of particular interest and concern.

Basically, a **Blue** is concerned about other people, so Blues will often see their top priority as the well-being of people in the company. They are interested in ways to improve employee morale and making the employees' jobs less stressful. Another Blue priority is the customer: customer service, customer perception, and customer satisfaction. Blues will tend to view change as more of a challenge than an opportunity and will be cautious rather than adventurous. Blues can be flexible about their priorities.

A **Gold** is often most concerned about the company's performance and financial priorities. A Gold personality might see the greatest challenge as meeting a timeline, a financial milestone, or a company goal. A Gold will prefer to adhere to established processes and worry about disruption to business-as-usual. Achieving consensus in the management team is another typical Gold concern. Golds will often express their priorities in a clear order and with specific time targets.

A **Green** personality will probably list multiple challenges, possibly with an emphasis on technology. A Gr een will be interested in finding the best solution to the problem, will look for breakthrough ideas in technology and process, and will want to be convinced that the solution will both solve current problems and meet future needs for the company. You might get responses that include several "objectively considered" alternative solutions.

Greens typically have informed opinions around technology choices but will always welcome more information. They will be prepared to take time to come to a firm conclusion. Greens will therefore be flexible about their priorities, and willing to revise ideas based on new information. Basically, Greens are concerned about being right.

An **Orange** personality will express their challenges in more personal terms. Listen to see if an adversary or competitor is identified where the challenge is to win against them. Oranges want to convince others that their recommendations are winners: "Is there a strong likelihood of success choosing this?" or, "Can this be implemented the quickest?" Oranges often express a strong sense of urgency. The Orange personality type is concerned about success and always looks for the immediate benefits.

Don't forget that the answers to the "what is the greatest challenge" question need to be taken in context and alongside the responses to the other questions. If you are talking to someone in a company that's facing severe financial difficulty about a solution that will allow them to implement a lucrative new product line, don't be surprised if the answer has something to do with revenue generation. Although that can be characterized as a "Gold" answer, in that situation any Personality Style might give you the same response.

"What's your approach?"

Blues approach a solution by seeking consensus from everyone who will be involved. They evaluate direction as a team and make their decision as a team.

Golds lay their approach out in a formal plan that includes a schedule leading to the implementation of the solution. Golds issue directives and will delegate assignments to others.

Greens will adopt a thorough approach. They will flag conditions to watch for and alternative responses to meet them. The Green approach is never cast in concrete.

The **Orange** approach will be easy to understand and the most straightforward. Oranges like to go from point A to Z as fast as possible, spending the least amount of effort and expense on the journey.

Observe in Context

How a person behaves and reacts to you gives further indications of their personality type.

Blues are warm and friendly and respond warmly to small talk about people and situations. They will try to make you comfortable. They tend to ask questions about the person and listen well.

Gold personalities are structure- and schedule-oriented—typically formal and serious. Golds will take positions of power or dominance. They tend to do the talking and come across confident. They will give and take in conversation and are more controlled. Golds hate to be interrupted.

Greens are succinct in conversation, liking debate and stressing logic. They are focused on the details. If you ask them about a technology item, they may respond with a fact or opinion. Greens are typically soft spoken and prefer to ask questions rather than do the talking. Sometimes you're not sure what they are thinking, as they display a "poker face."

Oranges are action-oriented and position themselves as the center of attention. They respond to small talk about sports or hobbies or anything action-oriented. Oranges dominate most discussions and love to tell stories. They are fast paced and energetic. Oranges are bold risk-takers.

How someone organizes and holds meetings is a strong indicator of personality type. A Gold is formal and aware of time and will express displeasure if promptness is not observed. An Orange might be multi-tasking during the meeting. Blues are not so controlled by time restrictions and can accept approximate start times and extend past stop times. A Green will almost always ask tough questions, often with follow-ups based on your answers.

In your first meeting with a customer, or before, you should discover their title or role in the company. This provides an important clue to their personality because personality types gravitate toward certain types of jobs. Don't make too strong of an assumption here, though, as you may find a Blue as CEO or an Orange leading HR.

CEOs, CFOs, and COOs are usually Gold.

Sales VPs are usually Orange.

HR reps are usually Blue.

CIOs, Engineering VPs, and engineers are usually Green.

How they are dressed will provide additional clues. Gold tends to look more traditional and formal, often wearing suits. Orange is trendy casual, wearing polo and golf-type attire. Blue is casual and fashionable but pays attention to color coordination and artistic style. Green is casual and comfortable, as if fashion doesn't matter. However, remember that people are a mix of the four styles; sometimes a person will dress to their secondary style (or even be dressed by a spouse). A stylish, color-coordinated, but frumpy dresser might be a rare Green-Blue or just a Green with a Blue spouse.

You also can learn personality information from the environment and surroundings where the conversation takes place. Meeting inside their office will provide a wealth of clues; observe the office decoration and contents to learn what they value.

A Blue's office may have a comfortable artistic look with artwork, music, family pictures, pet pictures, and plants. Their offices are relaxed and are oriented to make the visitor feel comfortable.

The Gold personality will be very organized and neat. Pictures could include symbols of "Leadership," "Perseverance," and "Teamwork." Books will include popular business bestsellers, strategy books, and organizational guides. You will most likely see organizational charts, mission and vision statements, and credentials like degrees.

The Green will have more of a practical tech look, possibly with gadgets, scientific themes, and technical books. Often the Green office looks cluttered to everyone else, but the Green knows where everything is.

The Orange personality will have family vacation pictures, team pictures at company events, or memorabilia from their favorite teams, personal trophies from sports, and performance plaques. Everything they ordinarily use will be close at hand.

Of course, everyone can have a blend in decorating their office, but the central theme often tends to lean toward one of the four personality types.

One last place that can be helpful is to look at their LinkedIn profile. The information there, including educational background, hobbies, and organizations they belong to, can give a hint to their style. You can even find other personality assessments that access a person's LinkedIn profile to determine their Personality Style.

Narrowing It Down

It's usually easy to get the customer down to one of two Personality Styles, such as when determining whether someone is left-brained (Gold or Green) or right-brained (Orange or Blue). To further refine your assessment of Personality Style, here are some subtle differences and similarities that can help distinguish which style you are addressing.

Golds and Greens are left-brain personalities, so they are both good with detail and problem-solving. Golds are more structured, whereas Greens demand their freedom. Golds do not welcome change as Greens do. Golds are better at managing time, while Greens respond to deadlines by working overtime.

Blues and Oranges are right-brain personalities. Both enjoy small talk, interaction with people, and a variety of social activities. You can tell them apart because Blues do not enjoy conflict, whereas Oranges will embrace conflict as a personal challenge. Oranges also have a competitive nature; Blues a comforting nature.

Golds and Oranges are bottom-line drive, concrete thinkers who want quick results. A difference between Golds and Oranges is that Oranges tend to be optimistic, and Golds are more cautious. Golds are usually thorough and organized, Oranges rarely so. Oranges live for the moment, while Golds are excellent planners. Golds are formal where Oranges tend to be casual. Both prefer to tell rather than ask.

Blues and Greens are intuitive thinkers; they seemingly understand something or leap to a conclusion without obvious antecedents in the conversation. They are more inclined to dive deep into a subject than Golds and Oranges. Blues and Greens are both slow to make decisions. A strong difference between Blues and Greens is that Blues like small talk and Greens are very succinct in their communication. Greens also like to debate, whereas Blues will avoid troubling topics. Blues will try to make you feel comfortable, and Greens can be oblivious to your comfort and emotions. Both tend to ask questions. Blues ask to learn about the person, while Greens ask to gain insight and information.

Both Greens and Oranges can appear to be confrontational. However, an Orange is challenging you as a person and potential competitor—but can easily switch to seeing you on their team. A Green is abrupt because what is behind you, your company's products and reputation, is more important to them than who you are. A Green might have trouble remembering your name.

Greens and Oranges enjoy their freedom and don't mind a lack of structure in a meeting. Both can handle debate, and they thrive in chaotic situations. However, Greens enjoy detail and Oranges are more interested in the big picture. A Green's priority is "ability," while an Orange's priority is "performance." Oranges make decisions impulsively, whereas Greens weigh the alternatives and so are sometimes slower to make decisions—but not always. A very bright Green can leap to a conclusion in an instant with reasoning that is not apparent to others. At other times, the Green could already have experience in the area, and rank the alternatives and form their conclusion before the meeting starts. A Green will have opinions that seem individual or even strange, while an Orange will have more mainstream likes and dislikes.

Both Golds and Blues will be engaging, but the Blue will be interested in who you are. The Gold will be interested in your status in the business and the community, and your performance. A Gold personality will establish that you are a good parent, while a Blue will be interested in what your kids look like.

Blues and Golds like security and safety and will resist change. They like when things are predictable and consistent. Conflict and chaos make them uncomfortable. The telling difference is that Blues are not as organized and structured as the Golds. A Blue will be relaxed and indifferent to how long the meeting takes. However, time is a priority to the Gold; they will be irritated if the meeting does not end on time. Likewise, when the goals of the meeting are accomplished, the Gold will wish to immediately end the meeting.

In summary, use what you've read here to help you narrow down the style of people you encounter. As you're learning, each one has distinctly different characteristics, even though we all carry a little bit of every style in us. The more you use the styles, the easier it will become to understand the style of others.

Real-Life Example

I had a sales call with a CEO in Dallas for the opportunity to speak at his annual sales kick-off meeting. As I always do in the first minute of the call after I shake their hand (pre-COVID, that is), I asked myself, *Who am I with? What personality might they be?* I started out by scanning the office for any hints. Sure enough, one of the walls had several pictures showing the CEO with some famous businesspeople and celebrities. I also saw plaques and awards that he had won for certain achievements. What Personality Style was I with? Well, most likely Gold or Orange. Gold since a majority of CEOs are Gold, and Orange since he had a "Wall of Fame" centered on himself and his company. Also, those Personality Styles are more common, so I had a higher chance of encountering one in the first place.

I noticed that he was dressed in a very nice suit that was kind of stylish and a unique color not usually seen with the traditional suits. *Maybe Orange? I thought. What else might give me a better clue to his style?*

He started out with an aggressive, energetic welcome, offered me a cup of his finest coffee—which he told me all about—and then invited me to sit down across from his desk.

His conversation started with how he'd found out about me through a friend at a network event. He then rattled off about twenty people he thought we both had in common as far as acquaintances at events, meetings, etc. Over the next forty-five minutes, he gave me the history of his career, his company, and his successes, and how he has exerted consistent influence in his market. What did I do? I smiled and nodded, smiled and nodded, smiled and nodded. The result?

At the end of the allotted time, he thanked me for coming in and really enjoyed the conversation with me. He decided that I was the right person to speak at his annual sales meeting, and I thanked him for his time and mentioned that I would send him my Four People Personality Assessment for the entire team of participants to take before the event.

The amazing thing about this sales meeting was I did no talking! I listened the whole time and made the appropriate gestures with eye contact and body language. Why did he approve of me without getting to know me?

The next day, I got the result of his assessment. He scored a 37 for Orange, which is three points away from a perfect score! I happen to be a 37 too. What does that mean? It's like a rooster on Ritalin! We love to be the center of attention, have no problem talking and dominating the discussion, and make decisions on gut feeling. We easily trust and put great emphasis on our network, who knows who, and go with other people's recommendations. What a great example of a meeting with a high Orange personality. His dress, the Wall of Fame, his high score all made sense. He wanted to talk, which is natural for an Orange, and I let him be in his comfort zone.

When you understand the Personality Style of your prospects and customers, it adds a whole new dimension to how you navigate relationships and sales situations. Keep the focus on them and what they want to accomplish—not you—and you will have much success! Now let's take a further look at the world of selling.

Next Steps for Sales Leaders

✓ How does the culture and environment of your company support the strengths of your salespeople's Personality Styles? Does your company support and work to build employee engagement? Is it structured with guidelines and rules, or is it more autonomous and independent in nature? Align the characteristics of the culture with the strengths of your salespeople to help them maximize how to work internally and reduce any frustration or stress.

✓ Help your salespeople use Personality Styles with their customers and prospects on sales calls to build long-term relationships. Review with them how to identify each style. The two questions they can ask to identify customers are, "What's most important to you when looking for a solution?" and "What are the greatest challenges from your perspective?" Their answers can reveal their Personality Style.

✓ Show appreciation for your salespeople's perspectives, insights, and contributions to the team.

✓ Remember not to stereotype a salesperson by their top Personality Style. Everyone is different based on their other scores, their background, and upbringing. Recognize that uniqueness.

CHAPTER 19

PERSONALITY STYLES BASED SELLING

Every company has its own sales methods and processes. You don't need a new one; you just need to understand how to make use of Personality Style insights to improve your success rate.

No matter how you handle the sales cycle, no matter what products, services, or solutions you sell, using the Four People Personality approach will help you in multiple ways.

As soon as you contact a prospect, you should identify the key decision makers and start to build relationships. So, what's new? Now, armed with the knowledge you have acquired about Personality Styles, you will start to identify the personality type of the key people in the customer's organization, and customize the way you conduct each step of the sales process to make good use of these insights.

The following chapters provide some practical hints for using Personality Style insights to help you:
- ✓ Connect with the customer and build strong customer relationships.
- ✓ Fine-tune your way of communicating with the customer to match their Personality Style.
- ✓ Understand and make use of different perspectives on needs, value, risk, and decision-making.
- ✓ Anticipate and handle customer objections.
- ✓ Bring the sales cycle to a successful close with a buying decision.
- ✓ Continue building trust even after the sale.

Understanding your own personality, the personality of others, and how these styles interact will improve your ability in each of these areas. An appreciation of Personality Styles provides insights into different perspectives on needs, value, risk, and decision-making. This casts new light on our sales techniques as we adjust our approach to work with each unique combination of preferences and attitudes. But this is not a rigid formula. Your customers are still people!

Understanding the customer's Personality Style will help you increase your chances of ***winning the sale, shortening the sales cycle, increasing revenues, achieving your sales quotas, and reducing sales turnover.*** These are the results every sales leader looks for!

CHAPTER 20

BUILDING CUSTOMER RELATIONSHIPS

Selling is about persuasion—convincing someone to adopt your point of view. Or, as a Blue personality would say, finding and meeting a prospects' needs. It's the transfer of emotions from one person to another. Whether it's convincing your spouse to go to the movies, your son to do their homework, or a customer to accept the terms of your proposal, selling is getting someone to *do something.* It's motivating another to take the action you desire. Selling is emotional because we make decisions emotionally and justify them with our logic.

Back in the mid-eighties when I was still new in my sales career in Alabama, I inherited an account from my predecessor. Anticipation of my first meeting with this company's president left me a little nervous because I knew that the most important goal was to establish my credibility and build trust. This customer was the largest in my portfolio, but they had the potential to be several times larger. My goal was to triple our business within three years.

During the first couple of months, my customer would test me on how well I could push our corporate teams to meet delivery dates. He kept track of how often I would follow through on his requests. He had me multi-tasking several issues at once. Fortunately, it was natural for me to let him know ahead of time if I couldn't live up to the deadline he wanted.

We had some frustrating moments. Yet after six months of managing this client's issues around deliveries, credit, new technology, and future forecasts, we built a long-lasting, trusting relationship that tripled his business in the first three years. He knew I cared about his success as much as my own. After a year on the account, he offered me my own office in his building. Basically, he knew I

"TRUST
IS ASSOCIATED WITH
HOW WE FEEL
ABOUT THEM
AND
HOW WE PREDICT
THEY WILL
BEHAVE"

worked for him, and he didn't have to pay my salary.

I didn't realize what Personality Style this customer was at the time, but I can look back at how competitive and go-getting he was and realize that most likely he was like me, an Orange. His secondary style was probably Gold. Our communication was direct, with no hidden agendas or motives, and I was able to say what was on my mind. He knew I would put his needs before mine every time.

After the first year, I was sitting in on the staff meetings and giving my feedback based on what my company was developing for future products. When the CEO had his fiftieth birthday, he invited me and my wife to join the celebration. When an order of twenty new computers was purchased during the end of our fiscal year (which helped me to achieve my quota), my company announced a week later a new product that came out with twice the power of what my customer had ordered at half the price. What did I do? I immediately visited the CEO and told him we needed to put in a change order to switch to the new product. For the first month of the fiscal year, I was negative $500,000 in my new annual budget. But I did what was right for my customer. Over the next twelve months, we generated more business than any other year in their history with our company, which more than made up for the loss associated with the change.

You cannot sell effectively without building sound relationships. Customers must know you well enough that they believe what you say and believe when you have their best interests at heart. Relationships are based on trust, which is developed over time. Trust between two people tends to be built up step by step, with each gradually accumulating more and more trust based on their experience of positive actions and trustworthy behavior.

Trusting someone is associated with how we feel about them and how we predict they will behave. Will they come through for us? Have they been consistent in what they have said and done in the past? Trust is also about our own level of confidence: have we done business with them before? The "trust' factor is more important than anything else. It's even more important than price. People often make decisions when they are emotionally driven by the salesperson or their company to do so, and a relationship of trust makes it so much easier for the customer to decide.

How can an understanding of Personality Styles help a sales professional build a better relationship? This is neither a trick nor a well-defined process. Your growing understanding of the Personality Styles and the temperament of each personality will help you in several ways. For example:

- ✓ You will find that you learn about your customer's values and preferences much more quickly. This will enable you to relate more easily and in a more meaningful way.

- ✓ Your new appreciation of the potential contribution of different Personality Styles will make you more readily accepting of differences and better able to communicate with empathy.

- ✓ You will discover that you will adjust your own behaviors and attitudes to align with those of your customer more closely. This will aid communication and establish trust more quickly.

Don't think of this as a mechanical process. Use the approach to help you relate to the customer, fine-tune your communication style, empathize, and build relationships. Sales success will follow naturally.

CHAPTER 21
COMMUNICATING WITH THE CUSTOMER

We all must **connect** with other people in both our personal life and business life. Good communication helps us connect with others. Poor communication leads to a lack of comprehension and lack of trust, which in turn makes it much more difficult to build a strong relationship. If a Gold real estate agent makes an assumption and says to a Green home-seeker,

"I know how important location is," we now know there is a significant chance they could misunderstand each other! Think back to the last time you and your spouse or partner disagreed over a purchase. Was it the item that was the problem? Or were you each placing different values and expectations on the potential purchase? Let's look at how personalities can impact communication.

Communication always goes two ways; it involves both talking and listening. A rule of thumb for salespeople is that your customers should always be allowed to talk more than you! The person who talks the most is usually least in control. Make it your goal to let the customer do **at least** 60 percent of the talking in a discussion. The more the customer says, the more you'll find out. It's almost that simple, but not quite.

We still need to correctly hear the **entirety** of what they're saying—what they intend to say, and what they unconsciously communicate by how they say it. We need to listen for two components: what is said (the facts) and how it's said (the feelings.)

Each of the four Personality Styles communicates differently. More than just the words they say, each approaches a conversation differently. The personalities of those involved in a conversation can affect not just what is said but also: the pace and tempo of the conversation; the intimacy of the conversational style; whether the conversation stays on track or wanders; and whether the tone becomes argumentative or amicable.

By listening carefully, we can gather clues about the personality types involved in any meeting or conversation.

Style of Communication

When we listen carefully, we can make a good guess about which personality group our conversationalist belongs to. This is important because we cannot just administer the assessment to everyone we meet! Even guessing their personality type can help us respond with what someone of that Personality Style would naturally expect. We can pace our conversational responses to their expectations, making them more at ease. By adjusting our pace and responding as they expect, we build trust; a customer will think, *She really understands me, or, He is one of us!*

Here is what to expect in communication style from each of the personalities:

Blues/Relators enjoy small talk. Typically, there is no sense of urgency when a Blue is in conversation about something personal such as friends, family, or a hobby. Blues will ask questions about you; they are interested in your answer. Blues have no trouble sharing a conversation, even if another person is talking more. Blues demonstrate sincere interest in what is happening in the life of their conversationalist. For Blues, developing trusting relationships is paramount, and this is apparent in the way they communicate.

Blues like the conversation to keep flowing and can talk about anything and everything. In fact, sometimes it seems that getting to closure on the conversation is not of much interest to a Blue. When talking with a Blue customer, make sure you have good eye contact. Blues are the best at reading body language. They listen to *how* something is said, not just simply *what* is said. Blues do not enjoy arguing or debate; it is best to avoid conversations where there might be strong confrontational opinions.

"BY ADJUSTING OUR PACE AND RESPONDING AS THEY EXPECT, WE BUILD TRUST"

Golds/Directors are more formal in their discussion. Golds always prefer to have an agenda when going into a meeting. I've actually put together an agenda for a twenty-minute meeting that had just three words on it—Introduction, Discussion, Summary—and the Gold client was pleased to see it! Setting expectations for a sales meeting is very important to a Gold. What is the purpose of the meeting and what do you expect to accomplish? There must be a purpose and reason for meeting. Make sure that if you have a set time for a meeting, you end the meeting promptly when the time is up. A Gold expects a forty-five minute meeting to last forty-five minutes. If the meeting looks like it might run over, ask the customer if they would like to finish the meeting or if would they prefer to continue. This will gain credibility with the Gold.

Golds don't like it when they feel their time is being wasted. Starting a meeting with small talk is acceptable only until they signal the meeting has begun. So, keep the small talk brief and get to your agenda. Keep your conversation moving and be concrete. Expect tough questions on the impact of your products and services on company performance. Golds need a *reason* to buy. Golds respect those who follow through on what they say they promise. Following up the meeting in an email or a letter will give you credibility and earn the Gold's respect.

Greens/Detectives communicate by asking many questions across a range of topics. Expect your most challenging questions from Greens. Keep your conversation succinct with a Green and get right down to business. Small talk is not appropriate unless the customer initiates it. With Greens, conversations typically are inquisitive, including many questions about the features of the products and services, how these will integrate into the business, and how these might be part of their business evolution going forward. Greens like to discuss and debate, often playing the devil's advocate.

Greens are visionary and always looking to the future. They can talk on the "big picture" level and then immediately dive into the details. Greens will test you if they have the chance, sometimes to display their knowledge and sometimes to establish your credibility. Many times, it feels as though there is a lot of resistance with a Green because the questions never seem to end. But questions are to be expected from a Green and this doesn't necessarily mean you are not making progress. If you are fielding these questions correctly, then you are, in fact, making progress in the Green's mind. When you do not know an answer, or are unsure of your answer, tell a Green firmly that you'll come back later with an answer. For a Green, that is much better than giving a fuzzy or evasive answer.

Oranges/Activators are entertainers; they love to be the center of attention. I sometimes joke, "When I'm done talking about me, I'll let you talk about me!" Let the Orange customer talk as much as they want. It's frustrating to an Orange when they do not get the chance to express themselves. Then this frustration can come out as a competitive challenge to your propositions. Small talk is expected and can range from family activities to sporting events to vacations.

Oranges are optimistic and high energy. Keep the conversation moving and active. Get them involved, excited, and interested as soon as you can, or you might lose them! Oranges are tough to pin down because they multi-task and stay very active. Oranges are impulsive and live for the immediate moment. More than others, they live on the edge—you must try to keep close to this edge too!

One of the exercises we conduct in our workshops is to ask each of the personality teams to write down the six words that best describe their communication style. One the next page is a list of words they can choose from.

Go ahead and select the words that best describe your style. Keep in mind that in a group of ten of the same style, the accuracy is much better, since their dominant style is consistent with all the participants, where your second style might bleed into the results when you do this by yourself.

The results are consistent when we conduct this exercise every time. Here is what you can expect each team to write down:

Blues/Relators – Open, Sincere, Purposeful, Genuine, Personal, Pleasant

PICK YOUR SIX

Fast-paced	Energetic
Optimistic	Sincere
Open	Pleasant
Structured	Personal
Detailed	Confident
Succinct	Curious
Expressive	Genuine
Persuasive	Inquisitive
Purposeful	Logical
Factual	Bold

Golds/Directors – Structured, Confident, Detailed, Factual, Logical, Purposeful

Greens/Detectives – Inquisitive, Curious, Detailed, Succinct, Logical, Factual

Oranges/Activators – Bold, Energetic, Persuasive, Expressive, Fast-paced, Optimistic

Notice the similarities with the Golds and Greens being left-brained and task-focused, and the similarities with the Blues and Oranges being relationship-focused. You can find skill cards that summarize the styles on our website: **_4peopleguide.com_**

Another clue as to someone's style is their tone and rate of speech. You will typically notice that Gold and Orange styles, being more aggressive, speak faster and louder than the more passive Blue and Green styles.

You can also identify someone's Personality Style by their style of writing in an email. Here are four real emails from friends that show their style. Guess which style they are, and I'll have the answers after you read through them.

Kimberly

Could it be that the bacon at the Hilton Garden Inn in Richardson is too good to pass up at 8:00 a.m. on a Saturday? Could it be that they want to hear the monthly speakers at our NSA North Texas meeting who they've probably known for years? Have they both let their gym memberships expire and it's a way to get a free workout in after the meeting?

As I am about to become the next President of the NSA North Texas, I have to be totally candid. I am juggling two nationally syndicated talk shows on NBC and a Forbes Nightly Business segment with a pending Forbes book. Throw in a speaking career that has me on the road so much my husband has had time to learn four languages. My non-speaker friends think I've lost my mind.

Lisa

To my dear friends. I am so amazed at receiving this award. Actually, I am shocked and at the same time honored. You folks are incredible. I view NSA North Texas as my family and value our friendships over the years as the best experience anyone can ever have. Thank you again for the honor and privilege of receiving the Charbonneau award. Love you all.

Vince

Gentlemen,

We will be starting the parade at 9:10. I'd like the following men stationed at the corner of Clear Springs and Woods. John, Kevin, and Steve. Please wear your orange vests and Watch Patrol hats. The parade should be passing Springpark Way and Joandrea and 9:17. The head police car should be 100 feet ahead of the cheerleaders. When we get to the clubhouse, please close the right side of the street. I thank you for your time and commitment in making this parade another success.

Sincerely,

Vince

Mark

Sorry for the delay—caught me with a ton on my plate with deadlines already in the mix.

Here are two logos that I redid based on the size constraints issue you needed—since the area they are telling you is closer to the dimension of a square than our initial logo (which is closer to a rectangle), I tried a few things to get within the parameter margins of what they are asking for—so, neither will be exactly the size they're requesting unless we totally redo the design.

Take a look at the two I did redesign but staying close to our original proportional sizes (height vs. width). Logo2 comes closest to their *parameters.*

If you don't like either let me know—I can create some others. If you want slight changes to these—let me know.

As for Keywords/Key Phrases, here is the list: [redacted]

If you see others you'd like to add—let me know and I'll add them to the website list.

NOTE: In this last email from Mark, I left out the list and some of the other details that were not relevant.

After reading the emails, the following are the Personality Styles: Kimberly—Orange. Lisa—Blue. Vince—Gold. And it should be easy to identify Mark, who is Green.

As you can see, after understanding the four Personality Styles, you can start to identify the styles even in an email. Remember that each style has a name that defines it:

Blue: the Relator   **Green:** the Detective
Gold: the Director   **Orange:** the Activator

Selling to a Blue Customer – The Relator

When selling to a Blue personality, remember to:
- ✓ Talk about people and their needs,
- ✓ Maintain good eye contact and
- ✓ Empathize with the customer.
- ✓ Be patient and show concern.

Selling to a Gold Customer – The Director

When selling to a Gold personality, remember to:
- ✓ Stay on the agenda.
- ✓ Give a good summary.
- ✓ Be clear on next steps and follow up.

Selling to a Green Customer – The Detective

When selling to a Green personality, remember to:
- ✓ Be calm.
- ✓ Invite questions and think through your answers.
- ✓ Do not get defensive with their potential skepticism.

Selling to an Orange Customer—The Activator

When selling to an Orange personality, remember to:
- ✓ Be action-oriented.
- ✓ Keep the conversation lively and moving.
- ✓ Give the big picture and the benefits.

The Business/Social Balance

I'm often asked, *"How do the different personality types view client entertainment?"* Well, each person has his or her own entertainment preferences and attitudes when it comes to socializing.

Can you tell who will be open to socializing and who will not? For the most part, the left-brain personalities (Gold and Green) are more objective and would prefer business first. The right-brained Blue and Orange, being more subjective, should be more open to entertainment to break the ice before getting down to business. Entertainment should never be an exchange of favors, but Greens and Golds might need to be assured that there is nothing expected in return.

While tastes vary, the Blue personality usually enjoys dinners and social settings that include plays, music, and the arts. The Orange personality is more apt to lean toward sporting events such as golf tournaments and ball games. Green personalities will also enjoy the arts but might only accept an invitation after you have gained credibility. Golds will also accept an invitation, but usually after you demonstrate follow-through by meeting prior commitments.

When it comes to building a relationship, which should come first: socializing or business? Should you ask for a business meeting to discuss goals or needs first, or can you start by inviting them to the theater or a golf game? I have met clients for the first time by inviting them to a golf tournament, and the relationship developed perfectly well from a first contact in this informal environment. While these clients welcomed the informal meeting, others might never accept an entertainment invitation without first meeting you in a business setting.

The key with entertainment is *not* to use it to convince customers to buy your products and services, but more as a means of building a relationship.

CHAPTER 22

CUSTOMER BUYING PREFERENCES

Why Do Customers Make Purchases?

What an important question. The answer is complicated, and never black and white. Customers are, of course, people, and people are sometimes unpredictable and awkward. That is why the business of selling is so interesting, challenging, and worthwhile! It requires us to release our focus and needs and to stand in the shoes of the buyer. Your ability to shift this perspective will determine your level of success.

A customer starts the buying process with both *business* and *personal reasons* for seeking a new product or service. Their assessment of value is determined by both *logic* and *emotion*, as is their assessment of risk. Their ultimate selection of a product or service involves both *objective* and *subjective* factors.

While we can never hope to predict the behavior of everyone with absolute certainty, the use of the assessment can help by providing valuable clues to likely behaviors and attitudes. But for this to be useful, we need to understand how the different Personality Styles perceive needs, assess value, view risk, and weigh up their options.

How Personality Type Influences Buying Decisions

The customer's buying process usually starts off with a perceived *need.* Different personality types have different perspectives on needs and will prioritize their needs differently.

The different perspectives on need are linked to different ways of establishing *value.* Something that is important and attractive to one personality type may be uninteresting to another.

"SELLING IS LARGELY ABOUT UNDERSTANDING AND MEETING THE NEEDS OF THE CUSTOMER. WHEN CUSTOMERS PERCEIVE A NEED, THAT'S WHEN THEY START LOOKING FOR A SOLUTION"

Different personality types view *risk* differently. Outside the business world, this is obvious: not everyone likes to bungee jump.

Different people use different kinds of criteria to make up their minds when presented with options. You will find that each personality type will be consistently linked to their attitudes about value and risk.

Clearly, your customer's Personality Style is the key to understanding how they prefer to make buying decisions. If you have insights into how the different personality types weigh needs, value, risk, and decision criteria, you will be better prepared to engage with them in a way that will influence their decision to buy—from you!

Needs

Selling is largely about understanding and meeting the needs of the customer. When customers perceive a need, that's when they start looking for a solution!

As you might expect by now, each of the different Personality Styles tends to have a different perspective on what their most important needs are, and therefore what they value most. Also, as I mentioned earlier, customers have both personal needs and business needs.

Business Needs

At the beginning of the customer's buying process, there exists an identified *business need* within the buying company. Customers purchase products and solutions to impact specific factors in their business model or to reach specific business goals.

Some typical goals are to:

✓ Increase profits and revenue

✓ Reduce operational costs

✓ Increase productivity

✓ Reduce employee turnover

✓ Improve cash flow

✓ Increase market share

✓ Reduce inventory

✓ Improve customer satisfaction

✓ Reduce product defect rates

✓ Reduce whole life total cost of ownership of equipment

✓ Improve corporate culture by supporting diversity and inclusion

✓ Bring new products to market faster

✓ Open new markets for products

Many business needs are tangible, and *objective criteria* are established to decide how the need will be met. If the business need is to lower product defect rates, the customer can measure the rate today and set a numerical target for improvement—say, a 40 percent reduction in defective products.

And their needs may also be intangible. This is when EQ can be valuable. It helps to build strong relationships within the organization and improves employee engagement, productivity, and morale. This will come across loud and clear in customer service and satisfaction. When employees are doing well, it positively impacts the customer's view of the company.

Most business needs are also openly expressed. The customer does not keep it a secret that, for example, the reason they need a new order handling system is to improve customer service performance. However, it's also possible that they don't know what they need. That's where a consultative approach using your Personality Style skills will help you to appropriately probe to learn what may not be obvious.

While as sellers, we'd rejoice if all our prospects and customers were open and honest about a need, that's not always the reality.

Personal Needs

Alongside the stated business needs, there may be one or more personal needs that will also affect the buyer's assessment of your offering. For example:

Will this product make life easier for me and for my team?

Will I get a promotion or a bonus if it turns out well?

Will it improve my visibility in the organization?

Will my subordinates be grateful and stop giving me a hard time?

Will this help me achieve my personal goals of professional growth, or other career milestones?

It is very important that a salesperson should know if a personal factor is likely to influence the decision, one way or another. There is no surefire way of uncovering this knowledge.

However, if you use your understanding of Personality Styles to help build relationships with the customer decision-makers, and with other people in the customer's organization, then you stand a much better chance of being seen as an insider and sharing in that less public information. If you are going to help your customer, you need to know their real needs.

Recognizing Our Own Value Biases

An eye-opening exercise in our workshop concerns "what you think your customer values." This exercise is done in teams, where each team is one of the four Personality Styles. We ask the participants to put themselves in their customer's shoes with the following prompt:

Imagine you are the customer and evaluating your own company for a project. Rank in order from most important to least important the top four reasons for doing business with your firm.

The table below contains the actual answers given during a workshop session for one of our clients, a telecommunications consulting firm. The answers are grouped according to the personality type of the team that provided the answers.

How the Blue Team Answers	How the Gold Team Answers
Good communication	Knowledge
Complementary skills	Meeting deliverable dates
Complementary personalities	Flexibility, dealing with ambiguity, adaptability
Creativity	Interpersonal skills
How the Green Team Answers	**How the Orange Team Answers**
Free thought	Required expertise
Correct, on spec, on time	Commitment to the client
Flexibility	Competitive price
Quality of product	Capability

The results of this exercise are crucial to understanding what each Personality Style values. Even though answers are never identical, we find there is a consistency in the responses every time we do it: each personality group is naturally inclined to list the items they personally value. For example, the Blues' perspective on what their customer would value is heavily slanted toward Blue personality characteristics.

Sometimes, as in this real-world example, secondary personality characteristics will trickle up, particularly when a participant is nearly balanced between primary and secondary styles. We see this in the Green response "on time," which is more typical of a Gold. Secondary characteristics are important.

Much the same occurs when we ask teams of real estate agents to go through the same exercise. Most often, each Personality Style starts with "location." This has already been drummed into them during basic agent training. But a closer look reveals that "location" has a different emotional meaning, and visual association, for all four personalities. A word may have a dictionary definition yet also connote different associations for different personalities.

For the Blue, "location" has a social dimension and means the "neighborhood." For the Orange, it's a house that is convenient to shopping and has quick access to major roads. For the Gold, it's a prestigious neighborhood that's close to the office. For the Green, it's convenient access to work and school.

This exercise reminds everyone that sellers often assume—wrongly—that their customers share their own values and preferences. Therefore:

You need to adjust your value discussion away from your own values toward those of your customers.

As you become more practiced, you'll be able to draw from your minor personality characteristics, to help identify and relate to what your customer would most desire—assuming you know the Personality Styles of the decision-makers you are targeting.

Just remember the best question to ask when determining the customer's priorities and value is: *"When it comes to purchasing _____, what's most important to you?"* Their answers will give you clues to their Personality Style.

Attitudes Toward Risk

When it comes to deciding, each personality has to weigh the risk associated with the decision. Each of the styles has a different view of risk, which affects how they will make a decision.

Some people will be satisfied with a small gain in return for a low risk of loss, while another personality will shoot for the moon, knowing the losses can be greater.

That's why it's quite common to see the Orange personality go into the relatively high-risk career of sales, where there is the potential for huge commissions.

Blues are typically risk averse. Blues prefer security and safety. For Blues, risk is directly related to organizational or social change. If we make this decision, will it be the right one for the people in the organization? What are the chances of failure? Is it a safe decision? Does it feel right?

Blues like to hear and then come to believe that the chance of failure is small or, preferably, zero. You need to establish trust and give the Blue customer steady support to move forward. You need to be there for them.

Golds, being left-brained, will be logical in their approach. Golds will only take a risk after they analyze the situation and weigh the benefits carefully against the costs and what the potential return can be. Golds make prudent decisions after assessing how the result of the decision will impact the organization and the company. What is the return if the risk is taken? Does the potential good outweigh the chances of failure and its impact?

Golds need a lot of valid reasons to make a significant change, because Golds view change as disruptive to the day-to-day operation of the organization. Golds also value security and safety. There must be an objective, solid return for taking the risk.

Greens will analyze the situation, and if it makes logical sense, they will often take a risk. For the Green personality, change is invigorating. "If we can improve something, we must!"

Being left-brained, Greens will make logical decisions using their ability to assess information and apply logic. Greens are more likely to be mathematically trained and therefore will see risk as quantifiable. For these Greens, risk is expressed as a probability and sometimes as a decision tree. The salesperson should be prepared to present objective evidence-based analysis of the risk associated with making the decision compared to the risk associated with not making the decision.

Oranges thrive on risk and welcome change. They do not see the potential downside; they see the opportunity for upside. Oranges enjoy the freedom of imagining many possible outcomes. They get excited when there are many different options they can leverage in a business situation; risk is less important than the opportunity for a positive outcome.

Oranges are optimistic by nature, so if they think they can win by taking on risk, they usually will. Being impulsive by nature, Oranges typically spend only a short amount of time analyzing a situation. Give them the immediate benefits of making the potential decision, and they are on their way!

A good example of how different Personality Styles view risk can be seen in how they approach investing in the stock market.

Blues might invest for social impact and because the company is humane, moral, or environmentally green, but otherwise, they will avoid risk by buying CDs and other stable government-backed investments.

Greens are more likely to be "value investors" or to follow a chart-based "technical model" of investing. They also tend to invest in what they know best, such as familiar technology or an industry they work in.

Golds tend to make more conservative long-term investments and would never invest in a volatile and risky stock. It would be common for the Gold to purchase a CD or tax-free municipal bonds.

On the other hand, **Oranges** don't mind going for the home run, fully aware that their investment is high risk but with potentially high reward. It is not unusual to see an Orange take the risk on a highly volatile stock in the technology market.

Matching the Value Proposition to the Needs and Personality

All salespeople have in their heads a set of value propositions for all their products, services, and solutions.

Based on our understanding of Personality Styles, we now know that different personality types see needs differently and value things differently. This means that we should forget the old idea that there can be only one value proposition for a particular product or service. A value proposition is a selling tool, and the value expressed must resonate with the individual customer to whom it's presented.

Since customers vary widely in their estimation of value, we must recognize that *each customer contact might need a new value proposition.*

Moreover, in some cases, such as selling a complex solution to a large corporation, several key people may have a say in the purchasing decision. For a project like that, you may have to produce a slightly different version of your value statement for each decision-maker.

This is not always easy. However, an understanding of the personality types provides you with a structure and guidance on how to do this.

Decisions, Decisions

When the time arrives, what criteria will each of the styles use to finally decide? Now that we understand the way in which each style perceives needs, value, and risk, we are starting to form a fairly clear picture of the ways that different people can move to one decision rather than another.

However, there is one more perspective on decision-making that is important to understand, and this too is influenced by personality. Some people tend to make decisions largely on the basis of objective criteria. Others prefer to come to a decision that is more subjective. Most people have elements of both objectivity and subjectivity in their make-up, but the balance varies.

To be *objective* is to attempt to eliminate emotion and bias from a decision. Of course, we are people, not machines, so we never reach pure objectivity. Nevertheless, in business decision-making, the aim is usually to decide on a course of action that can be seen by everyone as rational.

Subjectivity refers to our desires and emotions, relationships, and personal benefits. Being subjective means being distinctly personal in the consideration of factors: how does it affect me and those I care about? Sometimes one is aware of subjective influences and sometimes they are unconscious parts of our life. A subjective factor comes from the state we are in and the relationships to those around us. Everyone understands that subjective factors are personal and can therefore vary widely in intensity and importance from person to person.

If you are dealing with a *left-brain* personality type (Green or Gold) the decision will more often lean toward the objective, business aspects of your solution. Business needs will override the personal needs. However, if you are dealing with a *right-brain* decision maker (Blue or Orange), the subjective, personal needs can outweigh the business needs.

Common criteria weighed when deciding to buy a product, service, or solution are cost, capability, quality, and after-sales service.

Cost is the total cost of ownership (TCO) including the return on the investment. This cost includes the immediate price, the deferred downstream costs such as maintenance and service, and indirect costs such as any warranties involved.

Capability encompasses the features and functionality of the product or service and the technology that's used. "What is the product or service able to do?"

Quality is linked to the reliability and longevity of your product. "Will it last?" "Will it have problems?" "Will it consistently perform as promised?"

Service is how well you will take care of the customer if problems arise. "What hours are you available?" "What is your response time?" Service is all about your company's attitude on customer care and your ability to perform when issues arise.

Each of these factors—cost, capability, quality, and service—is measurable (and therefore able to be assessed *objectively*). However, what determines whether the level of quality justifies a particular decision? Even the most rigorous cost-benefit analysis may contain some subjective judgments. Without that type of formal rigor, we find in practice that each of the four Personality Styles, as they consider the solution you are offering, will give a different weighting to each of these factors, and that weighting may often be arrived at *subjectively.* Typically:

Blues give the most weight to **high-quality** and reliable **service.**

Golds focus on highest **quality** for the lowest **cost.**

Greens want **capability** as well as **quality.**

Oranges like low **cost** and attentive after-sales **service.**

These preferences reflect the value priorities of each Personality Style. To further complicate matters, additional preferences may come into play, such as the following:

Blues will consider the **impact on people** and **aesthetic appeal.**

Golds will favor a solution that offers **stability** and **order.**

Greens seek **novelty** and **innovation** in a solution.

Oranges will give extra weight to a solution that boosts **competitiveness;** being **up-to-date and cool** appeals to an Orange too.

Let me share a great purchasing example from many years ago with my son Bryan. In the summer before entering eighth grade, he decided to start his own business cutting lawns. I thought that was great and it would give him great experience with the world of business and sales.

Of course, the first thing he did was ask me to buy him a lawnmower. I told him that if it was his business, he would have to buy it. But being a loving dad, I said I would buy it, with the condition that he would have to cut our lawn first at no charge. He agreed.

We drove over to Home Depot for the purchase, and as we spotted the lawnmower section of the store, I saw my trusty "Murray" lawnmower I'd had in Birmingham for $129.95. I told Bryan, "There it is, my trusty Murray mower." Bryan responded, "But Dad, we need to get the Honda over here!" I checked out the Honda and it was $499.95. I told him there was no way I was paying that much for a lawnmower when a perfectly good Murray would do the job for almost a fourth of the price.

Bryan (who didn't know much about lawnmowers) asked the salesperson to help us out. The salesman explained that the Honda was better quality, had a terrific blade that chopped the grass so fine that it wouldn't be necessary to bag it, and the Honda would last much longer.

I, being an Orange, wanted efficiency at a low cost with good service, which I could get in Plano at the Lawn and tool store. And I like a deal. The Murray was my choice. Bryan is a Blue. For Blues, it's about high quality and service. After hearing the salesman and Bryan's persuasion (and he's good at that), I decided to buy the Honda, even though it was almost four times more expensive. Was it the right choice?

Later when I reflected on this experience, I remembered that when I had the Murray, every year in April the mower would need to be tuned up for $95. I noticed the Honda started every spring like it was just another day of mowing. If I looked at the total cost of ownership, I could see that the return on the investment was better for the Honda after just four years. Not only that, but the Murray's life expectancy was only about four years. We had the Honda for twelve years and it still worked just fine. A much better investment.

What we see here is the preference of the Blue Personality Style versus the Orange. The salesman convinced me that financially, the Honda would be a better investment in the long term. Understanding the personality of the customer can help you position what is most important to them.

We can see that just about any buying decision takes place in a rich and complex environment of varying perspectives on need, different concepts of value, a range of attitudes toward risk, and different objective and subjective criteria for selecting a winner. That's what I experienced in buying the lawnmower. The same can hold true for any purchase you or your customer makes.

Remember that everyone buys with emotion first. The right side of the brain makes the decision, and the left brain justifies it. The right side of the brain (the emotional side) is stimulated 3000 times faster than the left side (the rational side). That's how I decided to go with the Honda. Bryan and the salesman convinced me it was a better choice.

That's why people buy mostly on the referrals their friends make. People are influenced by those who have experienced success with a product or service. Many of us read reviews to help us make decisions. On Amazon, you might see ratings from a 1-star to a 5-star on the same product. And reading Yelp reviews of local restaurants will give you a sense about how people **felt** about their experience.

Now that you understand that each Personality Style goes about making decisions in a different way, you should be prepared to adjust your strategy with each customer based on your understanding of that customer's Personality Style. If there are multiple decision-makers, you can emphasize the aspects of value that will be important to each Personality Style involved—thereby covering all your bases.

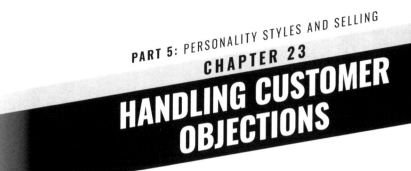

HANDLING CUSTOMER OBJECTIONS

Objections Are a Normal Part of Selling

Objections can frighten even the hardiest among us. But objections are normal and, if constructively handled, allow you to build stronger customer relationships. It is inevitable that in every sales situation there will be objections at some point in the sales process. Objections simply mean the customer is thinking of all possibilities as they consider your solution. Importantly, an objection also means you have their attention (a critical step) and they are interested in engaging in a dialogue (a critical next step).

Now you can work toward framing the discussion. So, expect and welcome the opportunity to move the sale forward by responding to the objections as they are raised. Of course, you must be prepared to respond confidently and effectively, in a manner tuned to their Personality Style.

Handling customer objections properly builds strong momentum toward success. While some sales training programs believe that objections can be completely prevented, I see objections as an opportunity to dialogue with the customer. The negative effects of customer objections can be minimized by focusing on the needs of the customer—and specifically, not pushing features that may not be relevant to their needs.

Never forget that you are selling to a person. Acknowledge and then respond to the objections raised by them.

The Four A's

There are **four steps in handling objections. The Four A's: Ac-**

knowledge, Ask, Address, and **Acceptance.**

Just as customers base decisions on both their personal and business needs, customer objections also come in two types— **factual objections** and **emotional objections**. The natural default depends on their style. You should anticipate and prepare for objections, based on what each Personality Style values. Doing so may help you prevent the objection completely. But if an objection does arise, you will be better prepared to handle it.

Whether a customer's objection is factual or emotional, you need to address the objection to move the sale forward.

First, you need to **acknowledge** the customer's concern. You can do that by simply stating: "I hear what you are saying," "I understand," or "I see." You do not need to agree with the customer, but simply acknowledge that you have heard their concern.

Second, **ask** a question to gain control of the conversation. Find out the reason for the objection and why it has come up.

Next you need to **address** the objection. If it's a factual objection, you must try to refocus or redirect the customer back to their most important need, which will hopefully outweigh the objection in terms of importance. If the objection is emotional, you must clarify or prove to the customer that their concern hopefully is not based on references or other customer feedback.

Specific circumstances, mood, and outside influences might determine specific customer responses. Your goal is always to provide answers to their objections. Generate emotions in the customer. Aim to satisfy their personal needs, which reinforce the customer's desire to buy your solution. Likewise, reinforce the idea that your product supports the business need, as weighted in importance by the specific personality type.

Your discussion with the customer will usually make it clear if you have addressed the concern in a way that is satisfactory to the customer. However, don't just assume that everything is resolved; you must ask for **acceptance:** "Are you satisfied with our answer to your

ASK FOR ACCEPTANCE: "ARE YOU SATISFIED WITH OUR ANSWER TO YOUR CONCERN?"

concern?" If you don't ask for acceptance, the customer likely will return to the same concern later in the sales process. If they are not satisfied with your response, ask another question, address their concern again, and ask for acceptance. Once they agree, the objection should be alleviated.

Objections to Expect, By Style

Let's take a look at the sort of objections that you can typically expect from each of the personality types.

With the **Blue** personality, expect more emotional objections relating to how the products or services will impact people's jobs, employee morale, and customer satisfaction. Objections are related to people and relationships.

> *"I'm not sure the rest of the team will be comfortable with this proposal."*

> *"This will really make our service reps unhappy."*

With the **Gold** personality, expect more factual objections related to the financial aspects of the solution. Golds will evaluate the numbers in your proposals with care and raise questions to establish credibility.

> *"Your ROI won't meet our investment criteria."*

> *"This looks like it will have a negative impact on our bottom line."*

> *"I just don't see how the productivity gains will be enough to pay for this."*

With the **Green** personality, expect factual objections around the capability of the solution, the technical aspects, the functionality, and where the solution might fit in to the overall technology strategy down the road.

> *"I think your competitor has a more advanced technical solution."*

"I just don't think you can achieve the expected performance using this approach."

"I'm not sure that your company will be around to support this solution in five years."

The **Orange** personality is a tough negotiator and places emphasis on the process of buying. They want to raise objections. Oranges also want to know the immediate benefits. Emotional objections are common for the Orange personality. Oranges like to negotiate since they view buying as a competitive game.

"I don't think you've tried hard enough with this discount."

"I'm disappointed you didn't offer us a better service agreement."

"I don't see how this will improve our competitive edge."

By understanding what each style values, you can now anticipate what objections they might bring up.

Facing Facts

Factual objections are just that: they are concrete and must be dealt with. Facts tend to be more important to those who are left-brained, **Greens** and **Golds.** Factual objections are often about the numbers:

"Your price is over our budget."

"The return on investment is short of our expectations."

"The terms and conditions need to include a three-year warranty."

Factual objections must be addressed head on, since they may point out where your products or services are missing the mark in a certain area.

Accept that a factual objection is *valid* from the customer's point-of-view. You'll want to deal with them head on, but do not contradict the customer directly or tell the customer, *"You are wrong."* Instead, leverage the Personality-Style weighted importance of business needs. As we mentioned earlier, a very useful question we can ask a customer at the start of a sales call is, "When it comes to investing in (the product or service) what is most important to you?" This will give you a good indication of their Personality Style. Now use this knowledge to **redirect** the objection with your response. Refocus the conversation or written answer back to the values that are important to that customer.

For example, if you have already discovered that the most important thing to a customer when buying a computer is storage space and speed, then an objection about price needs to be redirected back to the need for storage space and speed. *"Based on your priorities, I think you'll find that it's worth extra for superior performance and storage. For these features, you are getting the best price available."* Consistency is important to Greens and Golds. Remembering their prior answer about relative importance, lead with a question that they must answer in your favor to remain consistent: *"Which is more important to you, a lower price or the greater functionality?"*

Quieting Doubts

Emotional objections are more common from right-brain personalities—the **Blues** and **Oranges**. Emotional objections are windows into the buyer's doubts about a product or service, or your company's ability to perform, or the suitability of the solution for the customer's needs.

For example, doubts can be around customer service: "Can I trust you to follow through?" "Will you really be able to provide support to all our branches?" Or they may reflect concerns about the effort needed to implement the solution: "I'm not sure we can do this while keeping the old system going." These are emotional objections that require you, as the salesperson, to **clarify, reassure, or prove something.**

You must provide concrete reassurance that their concern is unfounded. For example, providing a Blue with a credible customer reference or testimonial that the Blue can identify with can go a long way toward quieting doubts. For an Orange, it's helpful to provide a third-party reference that makes it clear how the solution led to success or a competitive advantage. Factual case studies of previous implementations can help reassure doubters that your proposal is practical and achievable.

Well Done, Martha!

To further illustrate redirecting, look at how my wife and I ended up purchasing our dream home. When we decided we needed to move, our real estate agent asked us the key question, "When looking for another house, what is most important to you?" We told her that it was important that the house should have one story, and that it had to be on the Richardson side of Springpark. We knew what we wanted. Our agent found the property she thought was right for us. It met the location and was one story—but it was on the golf course, and the price reflected that.

We were tempted but responded that the house was a little big and the taxes were just a bit over our budget. So, here is an example of a factual objection to this house. It's a factual concern that the size of the house and the bills that would come along with it were over our planned budget.

How might a salesperson redirect or refocus based on the objection?

Martha, our agent, responded by reflecting back our expressed need: "You asked for a one-story house on the Richardson side of Springpark. This property is exactly what you asked for. Yes, it might be a little bigger and more expensive than you expected because it's located on the golf course, but it's the only suitable house available in the neighborhood you requested. This is a great neighborhood, and it might be years before another like this becomes available."

Martha reminded us that the location was our most important consideration. There was a real risk in not grabbing it. Knowing my Orange nature, she associated the decision as a contest I could win—get the house before someone else grabs it. Also knowing my wife's Orange personality, she pointed out how the layout and view of the golf course would make it a special place for entertaining our friends. Desire to stand out in entertaining is another Orange characteristic. Sold! Martha redirected us back to our main values, and the objection was gone.

Note that Martha not only responded to our specific objections but seized the opportunity to play to our emotional needs as Orange personalities: competitiveness and sociability. We ended up buying the house. We love our decision to this day. Martha did not manipulate us into buying; she understood both our factual and emotional needs and used this to respond in such a way as to remove our doubts and increase the attractiveness of the opportunity. Well done, Martha!

How could Martha have overcome this same objection for a different type of Personality Style—a Gold, Green, or Blue? With a Gold, she could have focused on the financial investment being a priority, and the great location of the house. With a Green, she could have highlighted the floor plan and the fact it is a one-story home. With a Blue, she could have focused on how nice the neighborhood is, the safety with the Watch Patrol, and the beautiful walking trails.

CLOSING THE DEAL

Moving Toward Closing a Sale

As you move toward what to you is a time for a decision, you need to encourage your clients or customers to maintain progress. But only if you have a strong reason to believe they are also nearing a decision. If not, it is time to step back and review objections and obstacles and the ways that your solution will help them succeed.

Remember that your customer's buying decision is linked to their needs and priorities—not yours.

How can you lead them forward while also providing your company with a realistic forecast? These are some of the strategies that will help:

Use the customer's perspective, not your own.

This approach will always be the most accurate. What you would do were you in their shoes is irrelevant, though it may feel most comfortable to you. As a sales leader, have you ever wondered why the forecasts provided by your sales team are so optimistic? Because they tend to forecast based on their own buying habits, not those of their prospect.

Understand the Customer's Buying Process

One of the most important strategic moves you can make is to learn how your prospect approaches their buying processes. Often what you see is just a portion of the full scope of making a purchase.

You might expect any or all of these during the process, especially with large organizations:
✓ Identification of needs and challenges
✓ Assessment of strategic options

- ✓ Detailed needs discovery and requirements development
- ✓ Budgeting the solution
- ✓ Engaging with decision-makers and their process
- ✓ Determining whether procurement is involved in the process
- ✓ Evaluating proposed solutions—both internal and external
- ✓ Making the purchasing decision
- ✓ Implementation
- ✓ Evaluation of how the solution is performing

Your relationship with the customer, enhanced by your understanding of the Personality Styles, will help you gather information about the customer's buying process, and at what stage of the process they're in at any given time.

Engage with the customer in the earliest possible stage when they are assessing their needs and budgets.

The more you understand their process, the easier it will be to uncover their real needs. That advantage gives you more influence and opportunity. Engage early in the customer's buying process. In general, if you only hear about an opportunity when the customer contacts you to get a quote, it's likely already too late.

If you've built a strong relationship and understand the process, you'll likely be among the first to hear about any opportunities. You don't want to be among the unfortunate who only learn about the RFP when it arrives in their inbox. Because, let's face it, rarely are the winners of the business in that position.

Consider the Competition

To fully understand the needs of your prospects, it's imperative that you know the competitive landscape. For larger prospects, take the time to do in-depth research on the trends and players in their sector. Your relationship with the customer will also help you understand their preferences and help you form an impression of your position vis-à-vis the competition. Often you will be up against not only the usual competitors, but an internal department within their organization who may also be considered a "supplier."

The common themes throughout the process of using the Four People Personality Styles are to: understand the Personality Style of the customer, identify with their values, and **build a relationship.** Using them consistently and effectively will help you successfully serve more customer needs, while helping you to achieve your personal and organizational goals.

How Much to Push?

As salespeople, we should always make the customer's needs our top priority. It's natural to think that our solution must be the customer's number one priority also! The customer might view purchasing our solution—or indeed, purchasing any solution—as a much lower priority. They have other things to do in their lives. The client's sense of urgency to award the business is seldom in line with our urgency for the sale. Many times, salespeople cannot understand why the client is taking so long to decide on their offer, the client simply has other internal and external considerations, pressure from above, and other projects to address.

A salesperson's desire for closure can sometimes cause stress in the sales-customer relationship, something always to be avoided.

Different personality types respond to pressure in different ways.

A **Blue** does not like to be pressured. Blues will take time to consult with everyone in the company who is likely to be affected by the purchasing decision. Until they are comfortable with the impact of the solution on the people in the company, they will delay making a decision. Pressing a Blue before he or she is ready will seriously damage the relationship between you and the client. To move a Blue closer to a decision, ask what else might help them move forward, and be patient. When you do attempt to close, don't ask Blues if they have decided yet; ask them if they are comfortable in moving forward.

To decide, a **Gold** needs to be very comfortable that the solution is completely right for the company: financially sound, low risk, non-disruptive, and using proven technology. Golds will work at their own timetable, no matter what pressure you apply. They have a step-by-step process, so the way you move a Gold toward closing a deal is to understand that process and support them at every step with the information they need.

Of all the personality types, **Greens** are likely to respond worst to pressure to sign a deal. A Green will be reluctant to make a final decision until all the facts are available, and they need to have a lot more detail than others. Until you are sure you have provided all the information that a Green needs, don't ask for a close. The best approach for moving the sale forward is to ask a Green: "What other information might you need?" and "What will be your next step in your assessment?"

Oranges respond more positively to pressure for a close than other personality types. Oranges may well be impatient to close the deal themselves because they are always interested in quick results, always keen to move on to the next new thing. If everything is lined up to make a decision, an Orange will not hesitate. So, the way to encourage an Orange to sign is to make it easy. Discover any objections and roadblocks and clear them away. Lay out the big picture, confirming that the solution makes financial sense. Point out the immediate benefits that will make the Orange look good in the company. And offer a great deal.

NOT JUST A THEORY

CONCLUSION

The Four People Personality Style approach is highly practical.

✓ It is a straightforward assessment that can be used by sales leaders and sales professionals in their day-to-day business.

✓ It is possible to make a reasonable and useful initial estimation of a person's Personality Style during a face-to-face encounter, without taking the assessment.

✓ The personality characteristics of each style make the method easier to apply and remember.

✓ Being knowledgeable about each Personality Style enables you to apply the information in real-life business and personal situations.

✓ After using this tool for years, I am more convinced than ever of its efficacy.

We have seen how a customer starts with both *business reasons*, and *personal reasons* to seek a new product or service. Their assessment of value is considered with both *logic* and *emotion.* Their selection of a product or service involves both *objective* and *subjective* factors. Sometimes it is difficult to determine what exact thought or attitude is driving a particular behavior. To do that, we would all need to become professional psychologists or psychics. For our purposes, this tool provides more than enough solid information to ensure that you connect better and improve your sales. All we need to do is become familiar with the important characteristics of each personality type, assess which style our customer is, and adjust our sales approach and communication style accordingly. Experienced salespeople already know sales success is based on having empathy with the customer and building a strong relationship. A practical understanding of the different Personality Styles helps you do that.

In closing, here are some reminders about using the Four People Personality Style Assessment in your selling career.

A complete understanding of the approach takes time and effort. If you are serious about it, buy the additional materials available, learn more, and work at it.

For an accurate assessment of an individual, he or she must complete the survey on our website: **_StuSchlackman.com_**. A casual assessment in the field without the formal assessment can work well but should be used with caution and consideration.

Use the approach to help you relate to the people you meet, empathize with them, fine-tune your communication style, and build relationships. Sales success will follow naturally when you can build deeper relationships.

This approach provides insights into what each Personality Style needs, values, their comfort with risk, and how they make decisions. But remember, this is not a rigid formula. Your customers are still people!

So now you know the Four People Personality Styles and have made them your good friends! We hope you've also learned some new things about yourself as you've read the book. As you grow to better understand the Personality Styles, you can apply the methods in your everyday life to strengthen your relationships and improve your performance in business. These friends will help you understand the perspectives, motivations, and attitudes of everyone you meet in life. As a result, you will become a different salesperson, manager, team lead, and friend.

Put this to work, get out there, sell, and succeed.

PUT THIS TO WORK, GET OUT THERE, SELL, AND SUCCEED.

Next Steps for Sales Leaders

✓ Coach your salespeople to understand what each Personality Style needs, what they value, how they view risk, how they prefer to communicate, and how they make decisions. Remember that Blue and Green styles are slower to make a decision than the Gold and Orange styles.

✓ Help your salespeople understand that the communication of a Blue style is open, sincere, and pleasant. The Gold style is more structured, confident, and purposeful. A Green style is curious, inquisitive, and detail oriented. The Orange style is optimistic, energetic, and focused on the big picture.

✓ Remember that customers make decisions based on their business and personal needs. Gold and Green styles place more weight on the business needs, the tangibles being more objective. The Blue and Orange styles place more weight on personal needs, the intangibles being more subjective.

✓ Remember that Blue styles are Relators, Gold styles are Directors, Green styles are Detectives, and Orange styles are Activators. This will help you understand your salespeople and their customers' perspective in any situation, and most especially in a sales relationship.

✓ Help your salespeople use the "four A's" approach to handle objections. Acknowledge, Ask, Address, and Acceptance. This approach helps them focus on the value the customer is looking for.

✓ The value of using Personality Styles in sales is to build trust-based, long-term relationships, win more sales and new business, shorten the sales cycle by better relating to the customer, all of which will reduce turnover.

ACKNOWLEDGMENTS

Writing a book is a huge commitment of time and energy and it would not be successful without the support of colleagues, friends, and family. I'd like to give a huge thanks to my good friend Ann Ranson, who has been with me on my journey, nearly since the beginning, as I invested in my sales training and coaching business. Ann has been my trusted advisor when it comes to strategic direction, marketing, and book writing. She has encouraged me during the ups and downs of our industry, and her friendship has been a blessing to me, as she has always had my best interest at heart.

Another special thanks to the North Texas Chapter of the National Speakers Association, which has changed my life as a speaker, trainer, and coach. NSA North Texas has been my professional family for over thirteen years and has helped me improve my profession in so many ways. The friends I've made have encouraged me throughout the years as we all share a wealth of information that we have learned from speakers around the country that have given their advice and wisdom to our chapter.

Thanks to my children, who have modelled success in their lives as they pursued their careers and realized how important sales is. Everyone is in sales in one way or another in their pursuit of success in the business world. I'm so proud of all my children in their careers and thank Greg, Rachael, Bryan, Jeff, and Kevin for all their support, encouragement and being there for myself and Betty in all we do.

Lastly and most importantly, a thanks to my wife Betty, who has been my pillar of encouragement all these years. Success in this business is not easy, and it would not have been possible without her incredible support. Her commitment and sacrifices in the beginning made it all possible. We both give the glory to God and His Son for all that has taken place in this blessed journey called life.

Stu Schlackman has been in sales and sales management since the early 1980s, eventually founding **Competitive Excellence,** a company that helps professionals improve their sales and business skills through workshops that instill "superior sales results." His first book, *Don't Just Stand There, Sell Something,* imparts wisdom, techniques, and practical advice for corporate executives, sales professionals, corporate trainers, and others who have the desire to compete and win in business and in life. He has also written *The 180 Rule for the Art of Connecting.*

Stu holds a degree in Mechanical Engineering from Rensselaer Polytechnic Institute and a Master of Business Administration from Kennedy Western University. He served as President for the National Speakers Association of North Texas for three terms and has also served the Leadership Richardson Alumni Association. He is a Certified Speaking Professional with NSA and has served on several committees. He is an advocate for the Leukemia and Lymphoma Society and was named their Man of the Year in 2020.

He has taught business courses as the Business Division Chair for Dallas Christian College from 2008–2009. Stu also has mentored students at the college. He has taught sales classes at University of Texas Dallas and has supported colleagues as a guest speaker at Southern Methodist University and Dallas Baptist University business schools.

Stu resides in Richardson, Texas, with his wife Betty. He has five children and seven wonderful grandchildren with potentially more on the way. Stu remains active in his community, business, and education, and is on the preaching team at Central Christian Church, where he has served as an elder for over fifteen years. He has also authored two spiritual books, as he grew up in a Jewish home and became a Christian. They are *From the Star to the Cross and Dinner with a Side of Doubts.*

Don't Just Stand There, Sell Something

The 180 Rule for
the Art of Connecting

Competitive Excellence was founded in 2004 by Stu Schlackman to help corporations, associations and organizations improve their sales and leadership skills for peak performance around the globe. Whether it's for team building or one on one coaching, Stu's company will bring your performance to a new height. The foundation of his work is based on the Four People Personality Styles tool he developed to build stronger customer relationships and to leverage the strengths of each and every individual.

Services Include

COACHING: Stu coaches to the specific needs of each salesperson to enhance their personality's natural style.

CONSULTING: After 20 years in corporate sales and sales leadership, Stu knows what works best for organizations. His advice has helped companies improve their effectiveness and increase their revenue goals by as much as 30% in one year.

SPEAKING AND TRAINING: Stu delivers presentations on over twenty sales topics from prospecting to negotiating and closing the sale. He delivers live and virtual events for every size audience.

Certify your organization with the Four People Personality Styles for sales, customer service and relationships, and well as how to work better together.

For more information contact Stu and his team at: StuSchlackman.com and Stu@StuSchlackman.com

Stu@StuSchlackman.com

Linkedin.com/in/StuSchlackman

Facebook.com/Stu.Schlackman

Twitter.com/Schlackman

Instagram.com/Schlackmanstu

BOOK STU to Speak for your Next Event:
StuSchlackman.com